CW00520704

Ailing Leaders in Power
1914–1994

Hugh L'Etang

The ROYAL
SOCIETY *of*
MEDICINE
PRESS *Limited*

Royal Society of Medicine Services Limited
1 Wimpole Street London W1M 8AE
150 East 58th Street New York NY 10155

British Library Cataloguing in Publication Data
A catalogue record for this book is available from the British Library

ISBN 1-85315-247-1

Phototypeset by Dobbie Typesetting Limited, Tavistock, Devon

Printed in Great Britain by Henry Ling Limited, The Dorset Press, Dorchester

Acknowledgements

First I must thank Professor Peter Hennessy. At our first meeting in 1989 he suggested that I wrote a third book on the effects of physical and mental incapacity in leaders. I also owe a great debt to Dr William Gooddy who described, and taught me about, 'brain failure'. Visits to the United States provided material unavailable in the United Kingdom. Colonel L Fletcher Prouty (USAF retd), once in charge of military support of CIA operations, and Professor Jerrold Post, founder of the Center for the Analysis of Personality and Political Behaviour, took me behind the scenes. Dr Lawrence Altman, medical correspondent of *The New York Times*, answered every request for more information about US presidents and presidential candidates. For 30 years Dr Humphry Osmond has sent me relevant extracts from the American Press together with his pertinent comments; Harry S Goldsmith, in spare moments from his unique surgery for paraplegics, has described his research into Roosevelt's final illness; and fellow researchers into presidential and other illnesses, Kenneth Crispell, Robert Gilbert, Robert H Ferrell, Robert S Robins, and Bert Park who is both a neurosurgeon and trained historian, have shared their knowledge.

I must express my thanks to many librarians and libraries: The Royal Commonwealth Society, the Royal United Services Institute for Defence Studies, the American Section, Senate House Library, London University, the International Institute for Strategic Studies, the United Oxford and Cambridge Club, and The University and The Cosmos Clubs in Washington DC. I owe a particularly large debt to the West Hill Library, Wandsworth, in south-west London, not only for its Metropolitan Collection, but also for the cheerful cooperation of all the staff who have fetched, carried and ordered books for me since 1961. I cannot find words to express my gratitude for the help and tolerance of my family; Cecily typed, re-typed and corrected successive drafts, Jacqueline, herself an author, encouraged me in bad moments, and Guy came to the rescue with urgent last-minute typing.

The book would never have been published without the interest and support of Howard Croft, Publications Director, Royal Society of Medicine Press. I am grateful to Yvonne Rue for her skilful editing and to Brian Weight for ensuring speedy publication.

Preface

The subject matter of this book is of as much importance to the general public as to the medical profession. Most of us are, to some degree, at the mercy of individuals at the apex of some organization whether it be political, commercial, bureaucratic or military. Few would deny that the mental and physical competence of these people is of importance to those in the organizations under their direction. Why then should not the mental and physical condition of those in supreme power be subject to review in so-called democratic societies?

Individuals who reach the top (or seize power) may be benign, wise and competent. Unfortunately some may be mad, bad or merely incompetent, and in a minority of these individuals performance will decline progressively through the onset of disease or age-related disability such as brain failure.

It is generally assumed that airline pilots and other responsible operatives are subject to regular health and competence tests and a fixed retirement age. But what of economists, industrialists, bankers and others whose personal competence is of importance to us all? There is a wealth of literature, biographical and autobiographical, which illustrates the catastrophic, predictable and preventable influence which medical and psychiatric problems have had on the conduct of business, finance, politics and war.

In the following chapters biographical information from published sources is used to illustrate the manner in which failure to recognize or deal with a variety of disabling conditions has influenced events. With advancing age, and for the most successful for whom there is no fixed retirement age, the probability of intellectual and physical impairment increases. As wealth and science permit additional 'spare part' surgery the function of original parts continues to decline until the subject becomes but a shadow of his former self. We surely delude ourselves if we believe that an individual who would be retired, unfit to run a professorial department at sixty-five to sixty-seven years, is considered competent to run a government or a multinational corporation ten, fifteen, even twenty years later, regardless of the support services at his command.

Discussion of such problems could only be permitted in an open and democratic society. It is fortunate that the only remaining superpower has begun to consider these issues. For those unfortunate subjects of bad, mad or incompetent leadership in an undemocratic society medical intelligence has little to offer.

Contents

Chapter 1

An Unsolved Problem

Sickness in the famous or notorious, the leaders in politics, industry, stage, screen or sport, alway catches the attention of headline writers and journalists. But whether the end of the story is happy or not the news soon slips from the front pages and public awareness. Publishers or editors would argue that there is no space, perhaps no time, for any evaluation of the significance, if any, of the illness or injury, its cause and relevance to the past and future competence of the patient. This is not to say that individuals have not made such efforts, sometimes in the face of criticism and hostility.

Even if medical evidence is available historians are still reluctant to assess the fitness of individuals, and any relationship between illness, decisions or lack of them, and subsequent events, on the grounds that their medical ignorance precludes judgement. A medical practitioner, on the other hand, who crosses professional demarcation lines and attempts such an evaluation can be criticized for not being a professional historian. Actors and actresses on the world's political stage are surprisingly discreet about the medical frailties of their fellows. When they break the rules of the club their evidence and opinions are revealing and alarming.

On 1 May 1957, for example, an article in the London *Daily Mail* included an illustration of a leading footballer undergoing a fitness test. Entitled 'should men who rule the world be treated like this?' Dr V V Tilea, the author, argued that never had the personal health of world leaders been so uncertain and never had world politics been, in his words, so troubled or unstable. As examples, he cited Sir Anthony Eden, the former British prime minister, who resigned because of ill-health in January 1957 after the controversial Suez war, President Eisenhower who had a coronary thrombosis in 1955, and his secretary of state, John Foster Dulles, who at the height of the Suez crisis in November 1956 underwent an emergency operation which revealed bowel cancer.

In Tilea's opinion it was not international problems which led to illness in world leaders but that illness itself was the prime cause of political instability. The ill-health of Eisenhower and Dulles was reflected, in his view, by their foreign policy. Their indecisiveness, postponement of decisions, petulance with awkward allies and lenience with the real trouble-makers resembled that of convalescents whose peace had been disturbed.

For these reasons, Tilea insisted, 'senior politicians and statesmen who bear the destinies of millions of ordinary people in their hands

1

should be compelled to undergo a rigorous medical examination before accepting office'. Candidates for the armed forces and civil service are not accepted without a medical examination and, therefore, national leaders 'should not be allowed to assume vital duties unless they are passed as one hundred per cent fit'.

This is sound medical advice coming as it did from an unusual specialist because Tilea was not medically qualified, but had earned a doctorate in another discipline. In international affairs, however, he was both player and spectator because from 1939 to 1940 he was Romanian minister in London where he remained until his death in 1972. His opinions were backed by forty years' experience in European politics and diplomacy so that his own observations on the relevance of individual failings would be far more extensive and practical than those of a physician who cannot directly assess a patient's behaviour or fitness between medical consultations.

Judging by the number of sick leaders since 1957 it is unlikely that Tilea's warning had any influence. An ambitious leader, greedy for power, regards illness as just another obstacle to be overcome and, if necessary, concealed. Disability in leaders can be hidden from the public by totalitarian regimes yet even in democracies, and despite widespread rumours or leaks, the electorate rarely expresses deep or lasting concern. Indeed, even when the details of disability in a leader merit serious attention, immediate measures to avoid either the repetition or the consequences of future ill-health are rarely demanded.

Tilea's message has been repeated in varying ways by a bare handful of medical authors. It has largely been ignored by historians, journalists and political commentators in the past thirty years.

Looking back, it is coincidental that, a few months before Tilea's article, Alexander Kennedy, a professor of psychological medicine, discussed a problem relevant to every type of manager, whether industrial, bureaucratic, academic, political or military. His theme was individual reactions to change[1]. He maintained that few individuals have the ability and strength to deal with every new problem and react, to use his term, as generalizers, quite distinct from the response of specialists in a limited field in which their training and experience may have previously confined them. He stated the uncomfortable truth, too often ignored or forgotten, that after age twenty-five there is a slow decline in speed of thought and capacity to learn. The best ideas are conceived before thirty-five and, after that peak, only maturity and experience can compensate for the progressive slowing of mental powers. In a rapidly changing world, in which leaders in any field rarely gain supreme power until they are in their fifties or sixties, the consequences of both mental and physical incapacity may be calamitous both for the leader who is no longer competent or the masses whom he supposedly leads or controls.

In 1993 there were several tragic reminders that the warnings sounded by Tilea and Kennedy, if indeed they were ever considered, had been ignored. On 1 May 1993 Pierre Bérégovoy, the Socialist prime minister of France from April 1992 until his party lost power in the March 1993 election, shot himself with his bodyguard's revolver. He had also served two terms as finance minister from 1983 to 1992. Exhausted by his years in office, depressed both by his delayed selection as prime minister, his early loss of office, and harassed by press speculation about a loan from a questionable individual, his end is understandable if not justifiable. Age was probably the most relevant factor. He was nominated as prime minister in April 1992 at the age of sixty-six, twenty-five years beyond Kennedy's level of maximum intellectual capacity and the ability intellectually to cope with change and adversity.

On 5 May 1993, four days after Bérégovoy's suicide, the body of Roy Watts, who had been missing for some days, was found floating in the River Thames. After a career as a British Airways executive, and a survivor of Lord King's reorganization in 1981, he became chairman in 1983 of Thames Water Authority in his fifty-eighth year. From this position he oversaw the privatization of the organization as Thames Water in 1989. Those at the top of many organizations promote the concept that management is an art or science of its own, which does not necessarily require detailed knowledge of, or previous experience in, the activity which they have now been chosen to control. For nearly twenty years beyond Professor Kennedy's age-deadline of forty, Watts remained in the familiar commercial, financial and planning activities of British Airways before serving as deputy chairman between 1980 and 1983. The management of an entirely new organization and staff, coupled with the unfortunate development of Parkinson's disease, may well have precipitated his desperate and final decision.

The problems of adjusting to change, which Professor Kennedy suggested could start as early as forty, are also sadly illustrated by the shortened life of Vincent J Foster, Jr. On 20 July 1993 the forty-eight-year-old lifelong friend of President Bill Clinton, was found dead in a Virginia park. On the evidence of a gunshot wound in his head, and a composite 0.38 revolver dating from 1913 in his hand, suicide was the presumed cause of death despite the apparent absence of any note and, indeed, of the individual who reported the fatality to the police.

As deputy White House counsel for six months he may have been exhausted after working up to fourteen hours a day, and depressed by media reports of the mismanagement of the White House travel office for which seven travel office employees were dismissed. In addition there had been comment in the *Wall Street Journal* to the effect that the White House was run by a 'clique' made up of lawyers from Mrs Clinton's Arkansas law firm. On the day he died Foster's wife said that he was having difficulty coping with office problems, could not sleep and was losing weight. A television programme later alleged that a document found in his office indicated that he was considering the possibility of consulting a psychiatrist.

Sometime later a note was found torn into twenty-seven (or twenty-eight!) pieces in his briefcase, leading to questions as to why it had taken so long to find. He wrote that he was not meant for the job or the spotlight of public life in a city where ruining people is considered sport. He admitted to blunders because of ignorance, inexperience and overwork but wrote that he did not knowingly violate any law or standard.

Although Andreas Papandreou would be failed for selection by Tilea and many others, he was elected again as prime minister by forty-seven per cent of the Greek voters in October 1993. At the age of seventy-four he may only be able to work for a few hours a day, and even that limited period in his suburban villa rather than his official office. His past history includes open heart surgery five years ago, his third marriage to a thirty-eight-year-old Olympic Airways stewardess, and a one-vote acquittal in the Supreme Court for complicity in the collapse of the Bank of Crete and of milking funds set aside for purchase of planes for the Greek Air Force. He immediately appointed his wife director of his private political office, his son as deputy foreign minister, his physician as health minister, and his wife's cousin as deputy culture minister.

Those who agree with Tilea and Kennedy may condemn, but cannot dismiss, a presumably democratic majority vote. Other candidates could have been even less fit, both medically and otherwise. The public is the jury and can make decisions contrary to the fine points of law, ethics and medicine. Unfortunately the public view is superficial; it is only a favourable image created by spin doctors and a media possibly controlled by proprietors with a personal interest, and even investment, in their chosen candidates.

Leadership by no means implies the survival of the fittest. Stress may well have been a factor in the heart disease sustained by Helmut Schmidt, Henry Kissinger and Alexander Haig, as it was in the tragic suicide of James Forrestal, once the American Secretary of Defense, in 1949. Swings of mood from elation to depression are usually associated with entertainers but they have occurred with far more serious consequences in political and military leaders, civil servants and even a member of the Central Intelligence Agency. Medical students are repeatedly told that rare diseases occur but rarely, yet uncommon blood disorders crippled President Pompidou of France and the Shah of Iran.

Steps must surely be taken to ensure that the subject of impaired leadership is taken out of the realm of medical curiosities and taught at Business Schools and Staff Colleges. An increasingly educated public throughout the world must be better informed by investigative rather than deferential journalists. Routine medical reports on leaders could be made available as they were by President Eisenhower and Prime Minister Begin. The health of candidates at elections can be publicly assessed, as was intended with Schmidt and Strauss in the German Federal Republic's elections of 1980. The London correspondent of Burda Publications generously provided background information on the health of both these candidates and accepted an article from me on the subject in August. The fact that it never appeared was not due to political objection or censorship. An explosion in a Munich beer cellar on 26 September which killed eight and wounded twenty-six was understandably considered even more important than an appraisal of the health of the two election candidates.

Public curiosity in their leaders should be encouraged and not suppressed since heads of state can plunge their people into disaster. Such curiosity can be condemned as muckraking though when applied to atomic physics it is praised as research. Admittedly Pascal dismissed curiosity as vanity 'for most often we only wish to know in order to talk about it'. And there is a curt warning in Ecclesiasticus (iii, 23); 'Be not curious in unnecessary matters'. Our fate is in the hands, hearts, glands, blood and brains of our leaders. Curiosity about them is very necessary for individual survival.

Chapter 2

Ailing Leaders—So What?

Illness in leaders is well covered by the news media although proprietors and editors risk being accused of pandering to the baser public taste and curiosity. It is true that those classified as 'the public' usually have an irreverent, even a ribald, attitude to their so-called leaders in every type of organization. Exposure of their mental and physical frailties is a confirmation of what they had long observed or suspected.

In contrast, members of that select network of political, military, professional or bureaucratic establishments tend to dismiss such revelations, possibly because a finger is being pointed in their direction. Indeed at the highest levels of government, command or influence there is an over-veneration of very important people. Crown princes or more junior contenders in the ante-rooms of supreme power treat their immediate superiors with a deference, even sycophancy, and regard their chief's conduct and any deficiencies as yet another official secret which must be concealed from both electorate and taxpayer who, in their view, are incapable of making a proper judgement about members of privileged and exclusive coteries. Even after publication of his controversial and much criticized medical history of Winston Churchill, Lord Moran emphasized that world leaders were exceptionally hardy individuals. Since he had written at great length on Churchill's physical disorders, from 1940 until his death in 1965, the hardiness and superior physical endowment of his patient were open to question.

Even by the 1980s with all the advances in therapy, mortality from a number of common causes was shown to rise steeply with advancing age. In considering the shelf-life of leaders, causes of death per million living in England and Wales in 1986 compiled by the Office of Population, Censuses and Surveys, can be compared in four age groups; 45-54, 55-64, 65-74 and 75-84. In these four age groups male death rates from all causes rose from 5267 per million living in the youngest age group, through 16 603 and 42 891 to 101 069 on the 75-84 year age group. Death rates from ischaemic heart disease rose from 2093 per million living in the youngest age group, through 6397 and 14 893 to 29 544 in the 75-84 year age group in England and Wales compared with 2016, 5827, 13 780 and 32 910 in white American males. Death rates per million for cerebrovascular disease increased from 261 and 996 to 3750 and 12 419 in the 75-84 year age group in England and Wales, and the death rates for white males in the USA were comparable at 167, 507, 1654 and 6012 in the oldest age group[1,2].

Similar increases in prevalence with advancing age can be demonstrated for chest infections, bronchitis, emphysema, asthma and malignant neoplasms including lung and prostate cancer. Comparable figures for disability are not available, though surveys conducted for specific purposes, for example provision of sheltered housing or nursing home accommodation, indicate increasing disability after the traditional retirement age of 65.

In the western world supreme power is acquired as early as the mid-fifties but the sharp rise in mortality, particularly from cardiac, cerebrovascular and pulmonary disorders, is the peak of an underlying, and often treatable, morbidity which can cause temporary or longer lasting physical and mental deterioration.

Lord Moran's remarks about the toughness of great leaders may have referred, not so much to their immunity from illness or disability, but rather to their determination and ability to overcome and ignore it. At first this may be a courageous and acceptable motive but it can result in increasingly disabled leaders weakly clinging to the reins of power but lacking proper control. Roosevelt overcame his paralysis from poliomyelitis to win the presidency; but his insistence on running for a fourth term in 1944 when he was also crippled by cardiac, pulmonary and other, even yet undisclosed, illness is questionable. Churchill was nearly 65 when he became prime minister and no doubt Moran was referring to his ability to withstand long working days and nights and dangerous journeys over the next five years despite a cardiac problem and pulmonary infections. It was far more difficult, if not beyond Churchill's capacity, to conquer his increasing disabilities between 1951 and 1955 during his second period as premier. Even allowing for improvements in therapy the health of those in Downing Street and the White House in this century is not outstanding. Sir Henry Campbell-Bannerman who became prime minister in 1905 at the age of sixty-nine had hypertension and cardiac asthma and literally died in office in Downing Street in April 1908. Henry Asquith who took over was only 55 but was faced first by bitter battles at home over the veto power of the House of Lords, the endemic problems of Ulster and later over the conduct of the Great War. His nickname 'Squiff' was more than just schoolboy humour because he drank to excess in public and private. His resistance to Lloyd George's campaign to seize power in December 1916 was also weakened by the effects of a respiratory infection and the shock of his elder son's death on the Somme in September.

Lloyd George was just short of his fifty-fourth birthday and until the break-up of the coalition in October 1922 his symptoms were mainly psychosomatic. During his years at the Treasury he had 'psychological chills' before budget day, neuralgia, neuritis and a clergyman's throat or laryngitis rumoured to be due to cancer or tuberculosis. He handed over to Bonar Law who really did have a laryngeal cancer. In great secrecy an exploratory operation was conducted in his west London house[3] and, as the diagnosis was not conclusive, the ENT surgeon took a furtive biopsy in Downing Street[4]. During the election campaign in November 1922 he had discomfort in his throat and speech difficulties and, although he attended debates in the Commons in April 1923, he could not speak. He resigned in May and died in October. Arthur Dickson Wright, the St Mary's Hospital surgeon, always insisted that he had a thyroid neoplasm. Sir George Newman, chief medical officer of the Ministry of Health, raised an ethical question when he went as far as to state that Sir Thomas (later Lord) Horder, who, incidentally acquired from Bonar Law's estate a second Rolls Royce, should never have allowed him to take office[5].

Stanley Baldwin, prime minister from 1924 to 1929 and 1935 to 1937, had no serious disease in office unlike James Ramsey MacDonald who served as prime minister in the Labour government from 1929 to 1931 and in the National government from 1931 to 1935. By 1931 when MacDonald was 65 he was publicly and painfully revealing signs of presenile dementia and from 1932 was further handicapped by two operations for glaucoma. Neville Chamberlain was sixty-eight when he took over from Baldwin in 1937 and, although his attacks of gout could not be concealed, there were no obvious ill-effects from what proved to be an inoperable carcinoma of the rectum until some weeks after he had been forced to give way to Churchill in May 1940. He rapidly deteriorated and died from acute suprarenal failure according to his surgeon, E. G. Slesinger of Guy's Hospital[6].

Churchill was in his 65th year when he became prime minister for the first time in May 1940 and for the next twenty-five years suffered the expected and increasing age-related disorders indicated in the American and British mortality tables already quoted. These included myocardial and cerebrovascular disease as well as attacks of acute lobar pneumonia. Moran describes many other disorders but never peptic ulcer which affected Clement Attlee, Churchill's first successor, in April 1951 after nearly six years in power. The rarity of peptic ulceration in world leaders is not surprising judged by recent British figures, for mortality is low compared with cardiac, pulmonary and cerebrovascular disease. There is also a possible reluctance to disclose this particular diagnosis with its tacit implication that the leader is failing to withstand the burdens of high office. Attlee then aged sixty-eight was the exception but he had to contend with the beginning of the Cold War, a weak British economy and internecine conflict in the Labour party.

Churchill's second and youngest successor was Anthony Eden, a mere 58 when he took office in April 1955, who was handicapped by an unpredictable obstruction of a surgically damaged and belatedly repaired common bile duct, medically prescribed benzedrine and his own self-medication, involving injections by his personal detectivo.

When Harold Macmillan succeeded Eden, on the latter's unavoidable retirement in January 1957, he was nearly 63 and after calming national and international ill-feeling caused by the Suez crisis won a great victory in the 1959 election. This was the summit of his achievement and, despite the winds of change, now hurricanes, in Africa, which he viewed with such benevolence, super Mac and his government sank in a series of seedy sex and spy scandals. In the summer of 1963 he himself noticed drowsiness. This led Dr Donald McI Johnson, Conservative and finally Independent MP for Carlisle, to question whether this symptom was due to a raised blood urea from renal failure due to prostatic obstruction[7]. Acute retention of urine in October 1963 on the eve of the Conservative party conference led to Macmillan's precipitate resignation before he could take the advice of his personal doctor who, like his patient, bitterly regretted the decision. Johnson told me that he wondered if Macmillan had a fear of taking professional advice since his teeth were noticeably decayed and neglected. Many doctors who attended the BMA annual conference dinner at Christ Church, Oxford, in July 1963 were alarmed at Macmillan's halting steps and physical deterioration when he appeared as University Chancellor and guest speaker.

When Harold Wilson became premier in 1964 he was only forty-eight. He came to power again in 1974 but resigned unexpectedly in 1976. Aged only sixty, colleagues noticed 'extreme weariness; the more exhausted he became the greater the flow of talk', its content revealing that 'he was living in the past'[24], a sign of an ageing brain. With the exception of James Callaghan who became premier in 1976 at the age of sixty-four and served a three-year term riven by industrial strife, it was an age of younger prime ministers. Both Edward Heath and Margaret Thatcher assumed power at the age of fifty-three.

In March 1981, seven years after losing the 1974 election, Heath cancelled his engagements for two months while he had treatment for what was called a glandular disorder. A 1982 profile in The Observer (July 4, 1982) claimed that he had been affected by an underactive thyroid for some years and that the signs were visible when he was prime minister. It was said that his mind wandered, that he was drowsy and that he fell asleep at concerts, dinner parties and even when talking to Henry Kissinger. In a biography of Lord Carrington published in 1985 Patrick Cosgrave wrote that at the end of 1973 and the beginning of 1974, during the miner's strike, power cuts and the three-day week, Heath 'seemed stricken in gloom and lethargy', his staff never knew when he would issue an order and his despatch boxes were returned without annotation of their contents. Cosgrave points out that the diagnosis of thyroid deficiency was not made until much later.

Heath's gloom and lethargy could be attributed to Britain's drift into anarchy. In response to a television programme in 1985 entitled 'Fit to Lead?', Heath wrote to the producers and denied that the thyroid disorder for which he was later treated had affected him when he was prime minister. A patient's own account of events cannot be ignored but the possibility of hypothyroidism in 1973 and 1974 cannot altogether be discounted. The early symptoms of hypothyroidism, tiredness, constipation, undue awareness of cold and stiff or cramped muscles, are not diagnostic, and may occur in fit individuals. More noticeable are the later signs such as slowing of intellectual and bodily activity, loss of appetite, increase in weight, dry skin, thinning hair, puffiness around the eyes, deepening voice, deafness and cold, rough skin.

As for Mrs Thatcher she showed no signs of any serious physical disorder during her eleven-year reign, merely the minor disabilities that inevitably arise with the passing years and which in her case were dealt with promptly and privately without months or even years on a hospital waiting list; varicose veins, a detached retina and Dupuytren's contracture, a fibrous thickening in the palm of the hand, involving the little finger.

Based on the mortality figures for England and Wales her freedom from potentially fatal illness is not surprising. In the fifty-five to sixty-four year age group, which covers most of her time in office, women when compared with men sustain around one-third of the deaths from ischaemic heart disease and myocardial infarction, just over half from pulmonary heart disease, slightly fewer from cerebrovascular disease and just over a half as many from cerebral infarction. In view of her operation for varicose veins, it is relevant that in the same fifty-five to sixty-four age group death rates per million from phlebitis, thrombophlebitis, venous embolism and thrombosis were forty-four and forty-seven—one of the few conditions where women are as vulnerable as men.

The American experience over the same period confirms that Lord Moran's faith in the innate superiority of world leaders was an illusion. Great men and women may be laid bare in the consulting-room but nowadays they play their parts with prepared scripts and suitable lighting on the world stage. Admittedly it would be impossible today for a hemiplegic and inactive president such as Woodrow Wilson to remain in the White House virtually out of sight, even out of mind, from the time of his stroke in October 1919 until, after completing two full terms, he handed over to Warren Harding in March 1921. He survived until February 1924 and outlived his successor who died, almost certainly of myocardial infarction, in August 1923 at the age of fifty-eight when the clinical signs were only just being widely recognized. Just as there was evidence of Wilson's arteriosclerosis as far back as 1906 when he was fifty, Harding's systolic blood pressure was known to be 180 mm Hg and when a later president, Franklin Roosevelt, then aged forty-nine years, threw his cap in the ring in 1931 and announced that he was a runner in the next year's presidential election, his blood pressure was 140/100 mm Hg and his electrocardiogram showed left ventricular preponderance and an inverted T-wave in lead III; in the days when there was no treatment for raised blood pressure a life insurance examiner would have viewed these findings unfavourably.

Eisenhower was sixty-two when he became president and, as might have been predicted from the figures, it was probable rather than possible that he would have both a cardiac infarct and a stroke. Kennedy was only forty-three when he took office in 1961 and had only recently been forced to admit publicly that he had Addison's disease. Not every aspect of his cortisone dosage, novocaine injections for spinal problems given by Dr Janet Travell and, more critical, the amphetamine (speed) injections given by Dr Max (Feel Good) Jacobson was fully revealed at the time. When Lyndon Baines Johnson succeeded Kennedy in November 1963 he had already had a myocardial infarct and during his five years in office, amid considerable publicity, had a cholecystectomy and simultaneous removal of a renal calculus in 1965. He would lift his shirt to display his abdomen and did so in November 1966 after a hernia in the abdominal scar had been repaired, apparently to distract attention from the removal of a 5 mm benign polyp from his throat. In contrast, details of the removal of a basal cell epithelioma from his left finger in January and from the outer side of his left ankle in October in 1967 were concealed until June 1977. Phlebitis, venous embolism and thrombosis is a minor cause of death, according to the British figures, but in the last hectic weeks of his presidency Richard Nixon undertook a Middle East tour despite severe thrombophlebitis in his left leg and the warnings of his doctor about the risk of pulmonary embolism. Indeed a few days after his return from the Middle East he left for a summit meeting in Moscow.

The presidential health record over the years is better than that of contemporary prime ministers. It has been said that President Nixon wondered how British prime ministers can stand the strain of their day-and-night attendance in the House, cabinet meetings and sub-committees, international travel, constituencies and above all, a stress not experienced by presidents, parliamentary questions.

A number of presidents appear to have escaped incapacitating illness in office including Calvin Coolidge (1923 to 1929), Herbert Hoover (1929 to 1933) and Harry Truman (1945 to 1953), the last two surviving to ninety and eighty-eight years respectively. Although Gerry Ford (1974–1977) was prone to falling down aircraft steps and Jimmy Carter (1977 to 1981) collapsed when jogging, these symptoms and signs were not of grave prognostic significance.

The innate, acquired or presumed health of leaders will always be a matter for debate and the Metropolitan Life Assurance Company attempted to answer the question. Statisticians studied the expectation of life for the presidents elected between 1933 and 1979 on the day of their inauguration compared with the American population[8]. The conclusion was that their expectation was 1.6 years less than white American males although, if the assassinated Kennedy was excluded, the expectation was 0.3 years longer. Since presidents and world leaders have long risked assassination, and as Kennedy himself understood that he had an illness resembling 'slow-motion leukaemia' but might live until the age of forty-five, the statistical validity of removing him from the 1933 to 1979 list might be questioned.

Other findings from the survey are also revealing. The vice-president's position in the United States is for obvious reasons not a satisfying one, for the only hope of advancement is to step into dead or disgraced men's shoes. John Nance (Cactus Jack) Garner, vice president from 1933 to 1941, said 'it isn't worth a pitcher of warm spit', while an Oregon senator regarded it as 'no better than a goddamned spare tire'[25]. T R Marshall, whose period of office from 1913 included the years 1919 to 1921 when President Wilson was incapacitated by a stroke, was more clinical. The holder 'is like a man in a cataleptic state. He cannot speak. He cannot move. He suffers no pain. And yet he is conscious of all that goes on around him'[26]. It has unexpected benefits, however, because in epidemiological contrast to presidents, they live 3.4 years longer than the average American, and Cactus Jack died two weeks before his ninety-ninth birthday. Even unsuccessful candidates for the presidency can draw some comfort from the finding that they live 0.2 years longer than their fellow Americans.

Despite ill-health many leaders reach and remain in their positions because, irrespective of any exceptional talent or even lack of it, the summit is their only objective in life. Indeed those who revere supposedly great men and women may admit their liability to the common infirmities of mankind but excuse any illness on the grounds of exceptional stress not experienced by the humdrum rank and file. They claim that a leader is continually 'on call' due to electronic communication and cite their exceptional exposure to the fatigue, time-zone changes and jet lag of trans-world flying to meetings and conferences.

Their hours of work admittedly are long and exacting but they have facilities denied to most of their fellow men and women; devoted staffs to sort their correspondence, write their speeches and, above all, a large and luxurious aircraft on call which relieves them of the common worry about luggage, check-in times, passports, customs, transport at the destination, and of the frustration of cancelled flights and even unavailable seats. As a result, their lavish support staff and relative ease of travel may enable them to attend important international conferences when they are not in the highest state of mental and physical fitness. Ordinary men and women who feel that they cannot surmount the fatigue of public, as distinct from private, air travel are fortunately also aware that they are consequently unfit to negotiate or to achieve any constructive goal at their intended destination.

Much is made of the exceptional hours worked by national leaders. This myth was shattered by President Reagan who had three-hour blocks in his daily diary free from work, early suppers on a tray at the White House looking at television, and long weekends at Camp David watching two films a night.

A leader's days and nights on duty may seem long but for many of their citizens the old-fashioned and regular '9 to 5' day in Britain and '8 to 4' day in America are gone. Blocked roads and worsening public transport compel individuals to arrive at work early and, inevitably, to stay late or later than before. President Lyndon Johnson's working schedule is reminiscent of Churchill's but whether he accomplished more by his long drawn-out activities is a matter for debate. Like Churchill there were periods of high and low activity and in Hugh Sidey's words: 'Johnson governs in spasms—he conducts great orgies of activity, either in response to a challenge or in support of his proposals. These are followed by weeks and months of quiet—times of brooding and evaluation[9].

Apart from the appalling inconvenience caused to his personal staff it is by no means certain that Johnson's protracted schedule was either particularly productive or that it could not have been compressed into a more normal pattern. He awoke at 7.00 a.m., had breakfast in bed, saw his special counsel and appointments secretary at 8.30, went for a swim at 9.00 but did not arrive in the oval office until 11.00 a.m. After morning appointments he had lunch at 2.30 p.m., then put on pyjamas and slept in the afternoon. He then worked from 6.00 p.m. until dinner at 10.00 p.m. Despite all his daily briefings he still watched the 11 p.m. news on a three-screen television console and then read in bed, presumably official papers, from 11.00 p.m. to 2.00 a.m. He certainly packed a good deal into the day and, typical of his life, he lay in bed one morning, dictating to his secretary, talking to his wife, and shouting at an aide whilst on the blind side a nurse adminstered an enema[10].

Unrevealed in the anonymous, official epidemiological tables lie isolated, even rare, illnesses which can incapacitate a leader or high-level negotiator but which can be long concealed from fellow countrymen and foreigners alike. The Americans are rightly proud of their open society and after President Eisenhower granted permission to reveal what some countries might regard as an official secret, namely his bowel motions after his myocardial infarct in 1955, the precedent has been followed in that country. President Johnson would bore his acquaintances with his current ECG tracing and nauseate others with the sight of his abdominal scar; the public became knowledgeable about President Reagan's colon; and every detail of President Bush's atrial fibrillation and hyperthyroidism diagnosed in May and June 1991 was not only revealed by his personal physician but his problems were openly discussed in the press by cardiologists and endocrinologists alike.

Not only is the American media open to enquiry and discussion about the health of the nation's leaders but the Central Intelligence Agency is rightly concerned with the health of foreign leaders. 'Rare diseases occur rarely' but, with modern drugs and techniques, the victims may survive long enough for their infirmities to cause both national and international ill-effects.

The fatal illness of President Georges Pompidou of France is an example of how evidence of ill-health is ignored even when it is vividly and visually obvious. Pictures taken at his Reykjavik summit with President Nixon in May 1973 revealed his puffy face and sagging, swollen cheeks and jaw just visible despite a scarf and overcoat. There were rumours of cortisone treatment for a blood disorder and an X-ray machine seen in the Elysée palace before his trip was mistaken for a betatron. His long illness has been carefully investigated by Dr Pierre Rentchnick who found a history of anaemia, epistaxis, raised ESR, increased sensitivity to cold and frequent infections. Some immunological disorder was diagnosed as early as 1972 which, in Rentchnick's view was Waldenström's macroglobulinaemia[11].

In 1948 Professor Jan Waldenström, a Swedish physician, described a malignancy of certain white (lymphoplasmacytoid) cells which secrete immunoglobulin M (IgM). Patients complain of weakness, fatigue, repeated infections, nose bleeding, visual problems, neuritis, dizziness, headache and temporary paralysis. On examination their lymph glands, liver and spleen may be enlarged while examination with an ophthalmoscope reveals changes in the retinal blood vessels found in conditions when the blood is too viscous.

Pompidou's condition deteriorated after June 1973 and he rested more, cancelled appointments, talked about death which he claimed was not far away. Diplomatic and presidential engagements were increasingly cancelled and on 29 March 1974 he had a retinal haemorrhage, epistaxis and rectal abscess. He developed high fever, lost consciousness and died on 2 April at the age of sixty-two. The infections, bleeding and mental changes could certainly have been due to hyperviscosity in his cerebral blood vessels and were very suggestive of Waldenström's syndrome.

For those who take comfort in the fact that political systems, efficient bureaucracies and devoted or critical colleagues can take precautionary or preventive measures, Pompidou's case is a terrifying warning. With its independent nuclear deterrent the use of the French atomic strike force lay literally in Pompidou's hands. There came a time when he could no longer remember the six-figure code number to unleash the force so the figures had to be marked on a metal plaque hung round his neck.

If more evidence is required for those who doubt the influence of ill-health on the conduct of affairs it is provided by the comments of Andrei Gromyko, the Soviet foreign secretary, on his meeting with Pompidou in March 1974; it was obvious that he was seriously ill, 'we were appalled by the waxy hue of his face', there was no hiding that his 'last weeks, if not days, were ticking away', and one noticed at times 'an unnatural concentration in him as if, although he was listening attentively, his inner gaze was directed elsewhere'. Gromyko admittedly conceded that Pompidou's intellect was 'as sharp as ever'[12]. Three weeks later he was dead. Gromyko's words, written fifteen years later, have the charitable tone of a discreet obituary notice. No serious negotiation or business can or should be conducted by anybody in Pompidou's condition.

Apparently unhealthy leaders can successfully conceal serious illness not only from the despised 'cookie-pushing' foreign diplomats but also from the more sophisticated CIA. The last Shah of Iran who died in 1980 at the age of sixty from some type of leukaemia, was the first to diagnose his own condition. On a ski-ing holiday in Switzerland in 1974 he felt a lump under his ribs on the left side which proved to be an enlarged spleen. Professor John Bernard, a French haematologist, was summoned to Teheran and he and Georges Flandrin found fifty-five per cent of lymphocytes (white blood cells) in a bone marrow aspirate and diagnosed chronic lymphatic leukaemia. They were asked by Dr Abolkarim Ayadi not to mention cancer or leukaemia to the Shah and the apparently more anodyne cover story was that he had Waldenström's macroglobulinaemia. Chlorambucil was chosen as the least aggressive treatment and he was given the tablets in a bottle with a false label. When the bottle was empty the valet re-filled it with the supposed contents which led in early 1976 to the Shah's rapid deterioration and the reappearance of an enlarged spleen and abnormal white cells.

From 1974 until the Shah left Iran in 1978 Dr Flandrin flew secretly to Teheran and, when he returned to France with blood samples, he attached the name and security number of an elderly relative, since this is a regulation in France[13-15]. It is clear that the CIA and British intelligence services were unaware of the Shah's illness.

Nor was the American embassy in Teheran any more successful in breaching the Shah's cover-up. Staff were more interested in his extra-marital affairs and even when news of his condition was leaked in an Austrian paper, and an Iranian contact reported the deterioration in the Shah's health, there was no further investigation[26]. It was not until October 1978, when the Shah's inadequate response to the opposition had become obvious, that the CIA asked for a full report.

In 1977 the Shah's ambassador in London wondered about the Shah's 'false priorities and disastrous economic policies, his military grandiosity and obsession with everything that flies and fires, his unquenchable thirst for flattery and his breathtaking insensitivity to the feelings of his own people, his vainglory and ceaseless lecturing—have these not dissipated any remaining reserves of national and international goodwill towards him?'[17] If pressed he, and other responsible western officials, probably would not even think or consider that such bizarre conduct, in what to them was presumably a fit man, were the symptoms and signs of mortal illness.

The innate or acquired superiority of leaders is widely believed and trusted, not least by the leaders themselves. Both in sickness and in apparent health few of their faithful supporters presume to question or discuss their accepted supremacy. The entirely different histories of Ronald Reagan and Margaret Thatcher bear this out and it is appropriate that their lives are linked by mutual esteem, even apparent affection, and also by a minor and remediable disability, Dupuytren's contracture of their fingers.

When Reagan was recovering from a serious abdominal operation neither he, his inner circle nor the medical profession seemed to be aware of the stark reality that he was not in a fit mental or physical condition to take vital decisions. Perhaps each party concerned thought that others would give appropriate advice. On Friday, 12 July, 1985 Donald Regan, the president's chief of staff, learned from Nancy Reagan that her husband needed surgery for a large intestinal polyp. Dr Burton Smith, senior White House physician was quoted as saying that what was variously described as a mass, polyp or lesion was the size of a golf ball which after scan and biopsy, according to Nancy Reagan 'had all the earmarks of being malignant'. On Saturday, 13 July, during an operation lasting nearly three hours, the suspicious mass, two smaller polyps and a section of large gut were removed[18]. Before the operation at 10.32 a.m. he had signed letters which authorized George Bush, the vice-president, to take over but by 4.30 p.m. he was 'alert and irrepressible as ever' and at 7.22 p.m. though still receiving morphine, resumed his official duties and signed documents[19]. On Monday, 15 July, the president was informed that there were neoplastic changes in the tissue which had been removed.

On Thursday, 18 July, the fifth postoperative day, Nancy Reagan allowed Robert C McFarlane, the National Security Adviser, to see the president. Accounts of this meeting inevitably differ. McFarlane claims that an arms deal with the Iranians and a possible release of Western hostages were discussed[20]. Donald Regan, who was also at the bedside, wrote in 1988 that there was a general discussion on hostages but, according to his notes of the meeting, nothing about exchanging arms for hostages. However, giving evidence before the board of the Tower Commission in 1987 Donald Regan confirmed the understanding about a contact with the Iranians and that the president said 'Yes, go ahead. Open it up'[21].

The meeting in Bethesda Naval Hospital on 18 July 1985 may have been permitted because of a naive belief in superman's invulnerability to major surgery, the custom that forbids a leader to step down temporarily or, more charitably, to lay ignorance of the debilitating effects of surgery and anaesthesia in a man who was then seventy-four. Bert Edward Park writes, on the basis of a Scandinavian study, that 'for elderly individuals in particular, significant cognitive impairment and memory loss occur during the first week after general anaesthesia, such that patients are routinely advised to make no major decisions during this time interval'[22]. Other studies extend the period to six weeks. If it had not been a matter of life and death in the Middle East certain of Reagan's activities could have been filmed for one of his Hollywood B-movies.

Margaret Thatcher is the very opposite of the president whom Simon Hoggart, when Washington correspondent of *The Observer*, called sleepy, hollow Ron. As prime minister her hours were those of Lyndon Johnson, 7.00 a.m. until 2.00 a.m. next morning, but unlike him she worked all day and night without any interval for rest or sleep. In June 1987 in her 62nd year she established a 20th century British record by winning her third election. The faithful at Conservative Party Conferences in 1989 and 1990 chanted 'ten more years' and she firmly reminded them that there was still more work to be done and objectives to achieve. Although women live longer than men only recently have some in Britain been allowed to retire at sixty-five rather than sixty, and Margaret Thatcher was ready and able to set new records.

Yet just after her sixty-fifth birthday in November 1990 her leadership of her party and government was challenged and she had no option but to resign with obviously pained regret. Her appetite for work and high office was not assuaged but she and her closest advisers could not appreciate that like other public performers, in politics, the arts or sport, she was 'over the hill'. The 1987 victory was the high point of her premiership and the next three years were downhill all the way. It was more than just the inevitable friction with colleagues leading them to be removed, shifted or to express a desire to spend more time with their families. It did not concern the British public that she was revered in the United States and Japan but disliked in Europe. What concerned them in 1990 were the side-effects of her last three years in power, the poll tax, changes in the health service, so-called educational reform and even, to her personal regret, the unfortunate consequences of her moves to change the allocation of television franchises.

A plausible theory was advanced in 1965 by William P Wilson, an American psychiatrist, to explain the sudden fall of great men and women. He called it Alexander's Syndrome after Alexander VI of

Macedon who 'when confronted with the problem of having no more worlds to conquer, sat down and wept'. Wilson paints a grim clinical picture of the condition; 'Its aetiology is success. Its major symptom is dissatisfaction. Its sign is beginning creative uselessness. Its prognosis is poor. There is no known treatment'[23].

It may or may not give Margaret Thatcher and other displaced leaders any consolation if they are assured that 'there is a lot of it about'. Most of us can contribute to our community and our country. Most of us must recognize that our powers are limited by time, circumstances, personal capacity or incapacity and the fact that every talent is exhaustible and limited. The addiction of power may tempt leaders to continue long after they have given their all. For the sake of their country, their people and even themselves steps should be taken or mechanisms made available to ensure their removal.

For those who belittle the value of investigating the rise and fall of leaders the case histories of Ronald Reagan and Margaret Thatcher are pertinent and should not be ignored. From a negative aspect it cannot be denied that Reagan, long trained at learning lines and briefs from the days when he was a film actor going 'on camera', was an important, perhaps involuntary, contributor to the Irangate disaster although later he may have forgotten, or been unaware of what he had been told.

Individual activity or inactivity cannot be dismissed on the grounds that it is not leaders who are responsible for historical changes but rather inevitable and impersonal factors of religious, social, economic and military affairs. Early in her reign Margaret Thatcher dealt with union dictators in the British coalfields and military dictators in the South Atlantic. In the late 1980s her driving personality could not allow her to consolidate her gains. It compelled her to seek and propound policies which, by their unpopularity, not only ensured her brutal removal from office but left her colleagues and countrymen to pick up the pieces and bear the cost of restoration. If Reagan at seventy was too old to become president in the first place Margaret Thatcher at sixty-five continued to be hyperactive and could not leave well alone. Many in the middle ranks of administration, bureaucracy, commerce or even the National Health Service will be uncomfortably aware of 'dynamic leadership' and the symptoms produced by this endemic state.

Chapter 3

Do You See But Not Observe?

It is fortunate that investigation into illness and its effects on leaders in any field does not depend entirely, as with most academically approved research, on formal records acceptable to scholars. Even if medical records are available access to them may be restricted and reproduction forbidden.

Other barriers hinder scholarly authors who wish to record the medicine of history. Doctors who advise famous, fashionable or notorious patients usually destroy their records when they retire. In some instances they use false names. More of a handicap, apart from the illegibility of the average doctor's handwriting, is the use not only of the usual medical abbreviations but of his or her personal shorthand which to the average reader makes the result resemble the hieroglyphics of an ancient manuscript.

In the 1970s it was possible for David Dilks, then professor of international history, University of Leeds, to study the appointment books of Lord Horder, a leading consultant physician during the first half of the twentieth century. He hoped to find whether or when in the late 1930s Neville Chamberlain, prime minister from 1937 to 1940, visited his consulting rooms. There was no mention of his name in the meticulously annotated books and of those listed only one was familiar; none other than Primo Carnera, a former world heavyweight boxing champion. Perhaps Horder's practice was less fashionable than commonly assumed but it left the possibility that some patients who consulted him may have had their names concealed.

Discretion on Horder's part could have been a matter of self-defence as well as professional confidentiality. A doctor who discloses, wittingly or unintentionally, the names of patients and the details of their illnesses faces grave charges and penalties. Morell Mackenzie, one of the founders of the Hospital for Diseases of the Throat in Golden Square, London, was invited in 1887 to examine the then Crown Prince Frederick of Prussia who was found to have a suspicious lesion on his left vocal cord. He performed three biopsies in May and June which were examined by Professor Rudolf Virchow, described as the father of cellular biology, who excluded cancer. In November a sub-glottic tumour was found to have developed and Frederick III, as he had become, died on 15 June 1888 after only ninety days as German Emperor[1].

Although he had been awarded the Comthur Cross of the Royal Order of Hohenzollen by his patient an official report from the

German doctors vilified Mackenzie who had been knighted by Queen Victoria in 1887, in part perhaps because Frederick was married to her eldest child. In self-defence Mackenzie wrote and published *The Fatal Illness of Frederick the Noble* in 1888 for which he was again vilified, this time by the British medical establishment. He was compelled to resign from the Royal College of Physicians and was blamed by the Royal College of Surgeons on the grounds that no provocation could justify publication of medical details about a patient. Only four years later in 1892 Sir Morell Mackenzie died at the early age of fifty-five years.

Not all was revealed at the time. In 1946 R Scott Stevenson, an ear, nose and throat surgeon, historian and editor of *The Practitioner*, wrote that there was 'more than a scrap of suspicion' that the Emperor's cancer supervened on syphilitic perichondritis of the larynx. Mackenzie later confirmed this to a personal friend in confidence. Moreover, four leading European laryngologists had agreed that the Emperor be given potassium iodide, then the specific treatment for tertiary syphilis. The smokescreen of cancer concealed a then unmentionable infection[2].

Victor Eisenmenger was another physician who wrote a book about the health of one of his patients. Two years before his death in 1930, Eisenmenger, an Austrian cardiologist who first described ventricular septal defect with an over-riding aorta, wrote a book describing his professional care of the Archduke Franz Ferdinand, heir to the Austro-Hungarian throne who had been assassinated at Sarajevo on 28 June 1914[3]. Not only did Eisenmenger go into considerable detail about the Archduke's tuberculosis, which apparently resolved after many years, but also about the hostesses brought to his houseboat, during his convalescence on the river Nile, whose rhythmic movements of hips and abdomen did nothing to conceal their plainness. The criticism of Eisenmenger may have been due to his lasting support of the Archduke and the denial of rumours that he had paralysis, 'softening of the brain' and mental derangement[4]. He may not have disclosed his patient's full history for Emil Ludwig, a German novelist and psychohistorian, refers to his 'unusually small pupils'[5]; a suspicious finding in an era when syphilis was as common as tuberculosis.

The rules about strict confidentiality in the doctor/patient relationship can be liberally interpreted by and between the good and the great. In a letter dated 18 January 1936 Sir Maurice Cassidy, a St Thomas' Hospital consultant, wrote to Sir Humphry Rolleston, editor of *The Practitioner* and agreed in a typewritten reply that he would 'be delighted to do my best for you' and contribute an article to a forthcoming symposium.

In his own handwriting on the lower part of the letter and on the back of the sheet he gave details of the current illness of King George V from which the monarch died two days later on 20 January. In the traditionally illegible writing of the doctor he described the King's drowsiness which had been worsening for weeks, causing him to fall asleep at table or desk. His peripheral oedema and cyanosis were more severe and he continued to be 'blue and breathless'. Cassidy imagined the outlook to be 'quite hopeless' but the King might last for weeks, though 'let us hope he won't become hemiplegic and aphasic and recover for a time'. His handwritten comments were marked 'confidential' but Cassidy surely should have assumed that the letter would be opened by a secretary[6]. His disclosure was unethical for, although Rolleston was a physician of the highest standing who could well have been called into consultation in this instance, he had broken the strict rules, both written and unwritten, of absolute secrecy about a patient's illness.

These rules about professional secrecy can also be conveniently ignored if the political climate or national interest permits evasion. In 1947 J R Rees, then an Army psychiatrist, and the other authors of *The Case of Rudolph Hess*, claimed that the publication of an individual's case history was unusual but not without precedent. After much consideration they over-rode their scruples as medical practitioners because of the importance of informing as wide a public as possible about 'the considerable abnormality of a man whose influence on world history has been marked'. In a world where psychopathic leaders can cause another war it is important to study such men and 'see how morbid fantasies can activate political conduct of far-reaching importance'[7].

Rees clearly felt he was covered by a letter from Hess, facing a possible death sentence at Nuremberg, granting permission for his clinical details to be released. Rees was unaware, as will be the rest of the world until 2017, since the offical documents are closed until then, that Hess, far from causing another war, flew to Scotland in May 1941 thinking he was on a peace mission although the previous messages to him from Britain had been drafted by our secret intelligence service.

No such licence was granted to Lord Moran, Churchill's personal doctor, when he published an eight-hundred-page book on his patient[8]. Churchill may not have had, as Rees attributes to Hess, 'considerable abnormality' but it would almost be an understatement to categorize him merely as a leader 'whose influence on world history has been marked'. Those survivors from the armed forces would have been most interested in Moran's account of his patient's medical history and behaviour; if only to understand, in the words of Correlli Barnett, the military and naval historian, Churchill's 'itchy-fingered interference with actual operation at sea'; 'the constantly changing operational priorities' in the disastrous Norwegian campaign and 'the fatuous expedition to Dakar' in 1940; his fantasy that sending *Prince of Wales* and *Repulse*, without an aircraft carrier escort, to Singapore in 1941 would deter Japan; and

his 'reversion to the *ad hocery*' of the 1915 Dardanelles campaign
in the disastrous assault on the Dodecanese islands in 1943[9].

In 1966 the British medical establishment, and much of the
medical and lay press were bitterly critical of Lord Moran (formerly
Sir Charles Wilson), Churchill's personal doctor from 1940 until
1965, and president of the Royal College of Physicians from 1941
to 1950, for writing his comprehensive study entitled *Winston
Churchill. The struggle for survival.* The motives of the critics may
have been mixed. Some may have been surprised and disturbed that
Churchill's physical and mental incapacity began as early as the
middle of the Second World War while his second administration, from
1951 to his reluctant departure from Downing Street in 1955, was
marred by progressive and noticeable decline. Critics of Moran, who
may have had no famous patients, and no stories to tell or sell,
preached about the confidentiality and even the post-mortem secrecy
demanded of the doctor/patient relationship. As many of the details
about Churchill's illnesses had already been published, Moran
should really only have been charged with bad taste and ill-manners.
He had passed on the non-medical details of private conversations
although they were not ethically confidential.

Moran was not apparently popular outside his own hospital,
St Mary's, where he had made considerable contributions to its
reputation and development. Indeed a review of his book in the
Evening Standard by Michael Foot on 24 May 1966 was headed by
his nickname which reflected the professional dislike, or perhaps
envy; 'Corkscrew Charlie sets the record straight'. The anonymous
review in *The Economist* was entitled 'The Fly on the Wall' whilst
a South African journal, *Medical Proceedings*, used the heading
'Moranography'. The weight of medical opinion against Moran was
publicly displayed, though his name was not mentioned, during the
annual representative meeting of the British Medical Association
on 5 July 1966. It was decided by five hundred and ninety-seven
votes to three that 'the death of the patient does not absolve the
doctor from his obligation of secrecy'. Whether the failings of a
disabled leader should be brought to public attention by a leading
physician was not discussed and the general tone was illustrated
by delegates who spoke of 'every Tom, Dick and Charlie' or being
'a proper Charlie'.

Lord Brain who had succeeded Lord Moran as president of the
Royal College of Physicians wrote a letter in his defence and asked
that, as the protests had by now been fully expressed, the affair
should be concluded. Brain must have been aware that in the case
of a less famous individual he could have been charged with a similar
breach of confidentiality. He had allowed Andrew Boyle, the
biographer of Montagu Norman, who had been Governor of the Bank
of England, to study his medical file between 1961 and 1965[10].
Norman had consulted Brain in 1948 and 1949. He died in 1950 but

it of course possible that Lady Norman granted permission for Boyle to see the notes.

There the matter lay until 1983 when the question of permanent, rather than a lifetime or designated period of confidentiality about any patient's illness, was raised. Dr Stephen Lock, then editor of the *British Medical Journal*, received a letter from the registrar of the General Medical Council, the controlling and disciplinary body, which stated that a recent obituary tribute disclosed confidential information which the writer could only have obtained in the course of a professional relationship. The controversial addition concerned Major-General Orde Wingate who had been killed on active service in Burma in February 1944, nearly forty years before. Lock was reminded that the death of a patient did not absolve any doctor from permanent secrecy and restrictions equally applied to doctors who received such information even in administrative or non-clinical duties. The inference was that medically-qualified editors, journalists or publishers came under this ruling.

The road to hell is paved with good intentions, wrote Shelley, and the editor's initiative was in order to explain that Wingate's attempted suicide in Cairo in 1941 was not just due to depression and imprudent self-medication with menacrine, as had long been stated by historians and biographers. The far more lethal condition of cerebral malaria was the cause of his disturbed behaviour and the corrective statements added to the obituary notice went far to explain his conduct and remove a permanent stain on his character.

Although the chairman of the relevant GMC committee admitted that the new evidence about Wingate might help to explain an unhappy episode he 'very much doubted whether such a departure from the rule was justified'[11]. It led Lock to ask in January 1984 if the medically-qualified historian was behaving unethically if he quoted the observations of George III's physicians or those of medically-qualified writers, such as Chekhov, Somerset Maugham or Freud, on patients who might be identified. Nevertheless in November 1984 the GMC accepted a recommendation that the existing rules on confidentiality should actually be extended to include medical authors, historians or journalists. The implicit threat to a scholarly investigation into historical figures was mildly softened by the acceptance that disclosure of information about famous patients 'long since dead' would not be considered improper; to beg the obvious question, 'how long is long?'.

Suppression of even the most trivial episodes in public and private life has become a British vice and the General Medical Council was following the trend. Fortunately its ruling about a patient's records is not too great a handicap for the medical historian. What the doctor sees and hears depends on when he or she is consulted and what the patient cares to disclose. In addition, as Sir John Colville pointed out in his criticism of Lord Moran and his book, the writer only saw

Churchill for short periods when summoned and not when he was in action during cabinet meetings and at international or other discussions when grave decisions were taken.

There is an even more important cause for charges of breaching confidentiality which medical historians must overcome if they are to avoid the paralysis of eternal censorship. In 1968 Dr Jonas B Robitscher, an American physician and lecturer in law and psychiatry, asked if British doctors who criticized Lord Moran 'were not in fact reacting to their chagrin' because 'they had not picked up the mouth droop, the unsteady walk, the slurred speech' of his famous patient[12].

While there can be little doubt that the mental and physical health of men and women in power are of concern to all around them and reliable information is subject to professional censorship, responsible citizens must use other means to discover the true state of affairs. The use of teleprompters, skilful camera angles, and editing of pre-recorded interviews are used to disguise disability but live coverage of events may reveal a very different picture.

Dr (later Sir Arthur) Conan Doyle based many of his Sherlock Holmes stories on his fictional detective's skill based on the actual practice of an Edinburgh surgeon, Joseph Bell. His torch incidentally has been handed down for today, at the University of North Carolina at Chapel Hill, Professor Mark E Williams, as a result of his Sherlockian reading when young, has long been 'intrigued with the specificity of personal information to be gained from detailed systemic observation', and teaches his students accordingly[13].

Consciously or subconsciously writers, journalists, Parliamentary lobby correspondents, politicians, bureaucrats, friends and enemies also indulge in 'detailed systemic observation'. Their scattered sightings when pieced together like a jigsaw form more than an adequate substitute, indeed may provide a clearer and more penetrating clinical picture and diagnostic aid, than that provided by the guarded and uninformative medical bulletins issued officially. In view of the careful selection, and indeed control of television interviews by VIPs, the voters and taxpayers should have their own Sherlockian curiosity and observations sharply focused by comparably observant historians and journalists. Only by such a combined operation can unfit and unsuitable leaders in politics, the armed forces and commerce be detected.

The shock and horror about Moran's book were naive for the author did not disclose, and may actually have been unaware of, the unstable side of the Churchill image. General 'Pug' Ismay's description in 1941 of Churchill's mood swings was a remarkable analysis by a combatant, not a medical officer. The medical notes in a 'fat folder' contribute little to this picture. On 10 October 1914 David Lloyd George, then Chancellor of the Exchequer, told Lord Riddell, a newspaper proprietor, that 'Winston is becoming a great danger' and likened him to a torpedo; 'the first you hear of his doings is when you hear the swish of the torpedo dashing through the water'. After the war, on 24 January 1920, Lloyd George in another letter to Riddell described Churchill as 'a wild dangerous fellow', reckless, indifferent to risks who 'thinks of himself before he thinks of his job'. A shrewd opinion in view of Churchill's letter to Riddell in July 1916 explaining why he had left the Army after only 80 days; 'I did not see why I should remain at the mercy of some 'ill-directed shot'[14].

No medical record could ever convey the penetrating examination of a future American president, then in his 57th year, by Gore Vidal, the American novelist, reporting the 29th Republic Convention in 1968;

> 'Ronald Reagan is a well preserved not young man. Close-to, the painted face is webbed with delicate lines while the dyed hair, eyebrows, and eyelashes contrast oddly with the sagging muscle beneath the as yet unlifted chin, soft earnest of wattle-to-be. The effect, in repose, suggests the work of a skillful embalmer'[15].

Nor could any IQ test or routine medical examination expose his mental limitations so starkly as his remarks on 20 January 1981 after his first inauguration as president. He was within two weeks of his seventieth birthday and would serve for another eight years. When the Speaker of the House, Tip O'Neill, pointed out that his desk had once been used by President Grover Cleveland and the new president remarked 'I once played Grover Cleveland in the movies'. The Speaker had to remind him that the character he had played was Grover Cleveland Alexander, the baseball player[16].

Press or lobby correspondents have repeated opportunities to notice abnormalities in the leaders whom they see and hear regularly. When they noticed President Georges Pompidou's grossly swollen cheeks at the Rekjavik Summit in May 1974 they realized that he was on steroids, as of course was President Kennedy. The White House press corps would regularly assess the mooning of Kennedy's face but in 1962 Charles Ritchie, the Canadian ambassador, noted another sign; 'I had not quite expected the waxy pallor of his skin'[17]. The penetrating eye of the artist may see even more during the hours spent with his sitter than might be expected. There were many critics of Pietro Annigoni's portrait of Kennedy for *Time* magazine. One doctor wrote that Annigoni had portrayed Kennedy 'with a cauliflower left ear, asymmetrical pupils, ptosis of the right upper eyelid, an eversion of the left lower eyelid, a hint of oedema in the left cheek'[18]. It was also noted that his left eye was off-centre[19]. The Kennedy medical records are still closed but it would be interesting to know whether Annigoni's interpretation was due to artistic licence. Despite their continued unavailability medical historians might hazard some other alternative diagnosis.

Idiosyncratic observations over the years by lay observers give medical historians the chance to attempt other retrospective diagnoses. President Raymond Poincaré's heart beat was so loud at a dinner in Paris just before the first war that it could be heard by the German ambassador's wife. Did he resent being the first President to dine at the German Embassy since 1870? Poincaré died in 1934 at the age of 74.

Richard Nixon's clumsiness and lack of manual dexterity has been noted by many observers. It may have lost him the 1960 presidential election. In August he struck his kneecap on a car door and the abrasion became infected, necessitating admission to the Walter Reed Hospital in Washington for leg traction. On 26 September as he got out of his car for the vital first debate with John Kennedy, he struck his knee yet again on the edge of the car door[20].

After the eventual presidential triumph in 1968 he visited Britain early in 1969, met senior cabinet ministers and spoke brilliantly. When coffee was brought in, leading to polite questions about sugar and milk, Nixon picked up, instead of his cup, a crystal inkwell and poured its contents over his hands, documents and the table[21].

When presidential gifts such as cufflinks, tie clips, pens and golf balls were distributed Nixon could not open their containers. Even though a bottle containing tablets was marked 'press down while turning' Nixon tried to open it with his teeth. When a pen was put out for him with its top removed so that he could sign a document Nixon would actually replace the top and then attempt to apply his signature. He would then remove the top but instead of signing the document would apply the nib to his left hand[23]. On other occasions he would bite off the top of the pen[24].

A distinguished neurologist at an American University is convinced that Nixon's clumsiness was a sign of minimal brain dysfunction (MBD). In many patients with this condition there is no evidence of structural brain damage but only of functional defects revealed by neuropsychological tests. Nixon's failure of coordination, also described by Fawn Brodie, can occur in those with MBD. She mentions his inability to dance, skate, catch a ball, swing his arms when walking, or change a car tyre[25].

Other characteristics which she lists are not uncommon in successful leaders in political and commercial life, and cannot necessarily be related to minimal brain dysfunction. Of Nixon's less pleasant attributes she lists political amorality, the capacity to bear grudges, needless deceit, lack of trust in others and a lack of conscience despite his talk of duty and honour.

If the clinical approach is used by commentators without access to secret medical records, it should be followed by statesmen and their bureaucrats as well as concerned members of the lay public.

Those interested in a clinical approach to public affairs should study the observations of Henry Kissinger during his years as Secretary of State. General Alexander Haig, then a colonel and military assistant to Kissinger, admitted that his chief had a considerable awareness of human psychology. Certainly, Kissinger's books contain examples of his clinical and psychological perception. He remarks on 'the occasional schizophrenia' of Chou En-Lai's presentation at a meeting, how the eyes of Andrei Gromyko, the Soviet foreign minister, remained wary and slightly melancholy and that Tito's eyes 'did not always smile with his face'[26].

He describes how Chairman Mao had sustained a series of debilitating strokes and could only move with difficulty and speak with considerable effort. Words, to use Kissinger's vivid description, left his bulk with reluctance, ejected from his vocal cords in gusts, each seeming to be a new rallying of physical force. At their last private meeting in October 1975 Mao could hardly speak and croaked sounds which his aides translated, wrote down and showed to Kissinger. In the shadow of death, however, his thoughts were lucid and sardonic, according to Kissinger. It is tempting to reflect how he would have described Churchill in 1955.

In Kissinger's opinion Leonid Brezhnev was both hypochondriacal and obsessional as he wore two watches, set to Moscow and Washington time, but could never remember which time was ahead or behind. Equally revealing are his comments on Moshe Dayan who had been Israeli Minister of Defence in the 1973 Yom Kippur war when he oscillated between despair and euphoria. Afterwards when he thought he was unobserved Kissinger could discern his underlying melancholy and frustration[27]. When President Nixon ordered the invasion of Cambodia in 1970 Kissinger fell back on lay terms when he observed that our leader had flipped his lid. Kissinger himself was worthy of observation since his fingernails were reported to be bitten to the quick and even bleeding[28].

It is frustrating to read the observations of another doctor manqué written just before his death. Dr Armand Hammer never practised and, from his account, his training as a medical student was minimal. Yet he saw world leaders and their illnesses in everyday surroundings, not in what some appear to regard as the secrecy of the consulting-room. His views about Russian leaders would have been encouraging had they been more widely known in the West. Such was Brezhnev's over-indulgence in food, drink and tobacco that Hammer gave him a book on diet and made the discussion of food and health a feature of future meetings. It was needed because 'his drinking was far beyond moderation or any sensible control', 'he was lacing into vodka at a terrifying rate' and on a holiday 'he drank so heavily that he had to be supported from the room'[29].

Hammer was shrewd enough to attribute some of Brezhnev's problems to hormone therapy for impotence. Allegedly he had

mistresses in many Soviet cities and consulted Dr Ana Aslan in
Romania for rejuvenation with a wonder drug called Gerovital[30].
Hammer surely must also have noticed Brezhnev's halitosis reported
by others[31]. Only Chernenko could drink level with him and, when
he died two years after Brehznev, it was rumoured that he had
cirrhosis of the liver. He also had emphysema and in December 1984
Hammer flew into Moscow to see him, accompanied by a professor of
pulmonary medicine. Chernenko's appearance would have deceived
the average observer because his 'slightly flushed face and confident
manner contrasted vividly with the pale, feeble figure we had seen
on television'. His shoulders were set square as if they had been
straightened by a coat-hanger creating a caricature of a military
leader. The pose did not deceive Hammer; 'This suggested that he
had to hold himself erect to breathe more easily and I could faintly
hear his lungs wheezing as he moved and spoke'. Chernenko's
physician declined any American help and denied any heart trouble
although two cardiologists were in attendence. Incidentally, the then
Dr David, now Lord, Owen on a visit to Moscow also diagnosed
Chernenko's emphysema.

Describing his first meeting with Andropov on 15 November 1982
George P Shultz, the US Secretary of State, wrote later that he
looked 'more like a cadaver than did the just-interred Brezhnev, but
his mental powers filled the room', and that 'he projected immense
intelligence and energy'[32]. Schultz's charitable view about apparent
illness may have been due to a personal mishap which could have
prevented him flying from Washington two days before. He choked
on an impacted fish bone which led to coughing and difficulty in
breathing. Despite Shultz's encouraging opinion Andropov only lived
until 9 February 1984.

Hammer's views on Tony Benn, a British Labour politician,
included a comment that: 'I found his eyes disconcerting with their
very bright and distinct separation of white and blue'; they were
'hard, bright eyes', with an '. . . intensity of focus'. In Hammer's
view 'eyes like those are the windows to a fanatical soul'. He was
disconcerted to see that Benn, an abstainer from alcohol, was
addicted to tobacco and tea, only removing a fuming noxious pipe
from his lips to drink 17 mugs of tea daily.

A snap diagnosis by a lay or even medical observer is based on
a fleeting impression which can only be confirmed or refuted by a
full medical history from a co-operative patient, physical examination
and further investigations. Kissinger was an unqualified practitioner
whose views and even turns of phrase on foreign leaders could have
been influenced by or copied from summaries by doctors and
psychologists from the Central Intelligence Agency. Armand Hammer
qualified as a doctor but never practised but both he and Kissinger
had lengthy meetings with foreign leaders and, even allowing for
personal factors or prejudice, were entitled to come to a conclusion.

What is not acceptable or excusable are the extreme views held by certain western leaders on their opposite numbers in the third world who, despite lack of precise evidence, they passionately love to hate.

School children develop an often irrational and unjustified hatred for certain of their teachers, fellow pupils or sports opponents from rival schools. Admittedly they may have clashed physically in classroom or games field. Yet world leaders can develop a personal hatred against foreign leaders whom they have never, or barely, met and spoken to. In 1981 key leaders in the western world began to hate Colonel Muammar Qadaffi and the views of former American presidents and top officials were listed by that distinguished American correspondent Joseph C Harsch[33]. The Libyan leader, according to Alexander Haig, then US secretary of state, was 'a cancer that had to be removed', while his country was guilty of 'unacceptable norms of international behaviour'. George Bush, then vice-president, said of Qadaffi that he was 'an egomaniac who would trigger world war III to make the headlines. He's the world's principal terrorist and trainer of terrorists'. On their way back from the funeral of President Sadat in Cairo, where they should have learned that Middle East problems were too serious for superficial diagnosis, ex-president Carter referred to Qadaffi as sub-human, and ex-president Ford called him a bully.

Dr Humphry Osmond, a British psychiatrist who has for long practised in America, classifies personality and types of behaviour and how, for better or worse, they influence negotiations. He wondered if any of the four Americans who used such puerile terminology had ever met Qadaffi and, if so, for how long, but he attributes the abusive terms to ignorance.

'It seems likely that the last three American administrations have been unable to fathom the Colonel and many of these undiplomatic remarks spring as much from incomprehension as from actual knowledge. Few of us are comfortable with what we do not understand. Is there any reason why the Colonel (Qadaffi) should be so opaque to so many able men who have great staffs at their disposal? There are a number of questions about the Colonel which if asked could be answered'[34].

What Osmond could not be expected to know was that in January 1981 a CIA psychologist had provided William Casey, director of central intelligence, with a psychological profile of Qadaffi. As a child the Libyan leader had absorbed the Bedouin characteristics of naive idealism, religious fanaticism, pride, austerity, fear of and aversion to strangers and foreigners, and deep sensitivity. Because of discrimination against Bedouins by urbanized Libyans in city schools

Qadaffi disliked elite societies, followed Bedouin customs and developed a feeling for the underprivileged. As a result he rebelled against authority at home and abroad and, in self-defence, had developed 'an exalted, grandiose self-importance'.

The US intelligence branches complained that the psychological profiles were not good enough and relied on clichés. One such profile from Dr Jerrold Post, head of the CIA political psychological division, had stated:

> 'Despite popular belief to the contrary, Qadaffi is not psychotic, and for the most part is in contact with reality. . . . (he) is judged to suffer from a severe personality disturbance—a "borderline personality disorder" '[35].

In this or another report it was stated that 'under severe stress, he (Qadaffi) is subject to episodes of bizarre behaviour when his judgement may be faulty'. Like Ford, Carter, Nixon and Haig, Post may never have had personal contact with Qadaffi, but in view of their ignorance of his background and psychology these professional views may have been kept from them. Indeed to reduce the Great Libyan Dictator to a human, understandable level was dismissed as silliness by Geoffrey Kemp, the national security council's expert on the Middle East and South Asia, who even suggested that a novelist be recruited to assist with the profiles.

During Reagan's reign Qadaffi was not upgraded to be the Great Satan nor was Libya classified as another Evil Empire. Nevertheless supposedly responsible leaders from the first and allegedly civilized and educated world, despite professional advice to the contrary, developed, in what charitably might be called ignorance, unfounded, distorted and even dangerous attitudes about those who in their minds were enemies, with resulting threats to world peace and stability. Should those who are susceptible to what are excused as 'gut reactions' be themselves subject to psychological assessment? A wider appraisal of foreign leaders is highly desirable but it must be carried out with professional, even judicial, detachment. Describing a meeting with Ferdinand Marcos, Admiral Crowe, then commander-in-chief Pacific (CINCPAC) posed the question 'was he alert or woozy? Sometimes his eyes were glazed over and he was barely able to speak'[36]. Only a trained physician could provide an opinion or answer.

Denigration of psychiatric profiles may be prompted by fear of their application to home officials as well as enemies. In 1990 Saddam Hussein was widely regarded as erratic, eccentric or mad. Dr Post argued that far from being a psychotic megalomaniac he was rational but dangerous. If he sees a way out, he will take it, wait patiently and strike again later[38]. 'Psychobabble' was the opinion of President Bush's aides who found that Saddam's profile was of little help during the Gulf crisis. Such profiles are questioned because the authors 'seek to psychoanalyze from afar, blending political science with psychology in a hybrid science or art'. Robert Gates, a former Director of Central Intelligence was dismissive: 'Trying to diagnose somebody from 5000 miles away whom you've never met does not fill me with confidence'[39].

Remote-control diagnosis has limitations. In gathering evidence about well-protected, even concealed, leaders, on the spot observers, whether doctors, journalists, diplomats or undercover agents, must develop their powers of observation and at least one eye for the unusual. Even experienced clinicians can miss vital clues in the patient's medical history and appearance. When the US Secretary of State, George Shultz, met the Soviet premier, Nikolai Tikonov in 1984 he was told that the Russian was 'an old, doddering man holding a ceremonial post and out of the action'. In came 'a bouncy, lively individual, fully prepared to debate me energetically'[32]. Acute observation of, and deduction about, key individuals are essential at home as well as abroad.

The early clues to medical diagnosis are given in a patient's daily life, often months before a diagnosis is made in consulting-room or hospital. In October 1990 Brent Scowcroft, the National Security adviser, spoke to Bob Woodward of *The Washington Post*. He was finding it difficult 'to manage and control an incredibly active President'[37]. Bush was out making statements, giving press conferences almost daily, up at dawn making calls, on the phone with one world leader after another, setting up meetings. On a relaxing weekend 'Bush talked with or saw more people related to his job than most people did in a normal work week'.

Woodward did not publish this account until 1991 but a report in *The New York Times* on 9 December 1990 was, unconsciously perhaps, diagnostic. At a news conference during Bush's tour of Latin America reporter Maureen Dowd studied what she described as the 'hyperactive Bush' who at news conferences made faces, grinned, gesticulated, squirmed and chatted while questions and answers were translated for the local and American press corps. Bush checked his watch, compared schedules with other leaders, mouthed messages to reporters, put mints into his mouth and took them out again and put them into his pocket when it was time to speak. He also poured water for himself or asked for more coffee and, in Argentina, actually opened the lid of the podium where he was sitting to look underneath.

In view of this it should not have been a surprise that in May 1991 Bush developed atrial fibrillation which, after investigation, was attributed to hyperthyroidism. The restlessness together with the mental and physical hyperactivity noted by astute reporters were retrospectively diagnostic and speculative, leading William Safire of *The New York Times* to pose questions about the state of the presidential thyroid when the Gulf War was launched in August

1990 and abruptly stopped in March 1991, when the Kurds and
Muslims opposed to Saddam were abandoned to their fate. The onset
of the atrial fibrillation may be significant or a coincidence for, as
Jeff Postlewaite of *The Independent* pointed out, it occurred a few
days after Bush had denied delaying the release of the American
hostages in Iran during the 1980 campaign when he became vice-
president and Reagan president.

  'Eternal vigilance is the price of liberty' sums up the words of John
Philpot Curran 200 years ago; the word survival might be
substituted today for liberty. Vigilance about leaders in any field
can be regarded either as muck-raking journalism or the academic
scholarship of medical historians. Vigilance and curiosity about
world leaders, who can avoid contact with their people for security
reasons but cannot avoid TV exposures, may lead to an earlier
awareness of any oddity or abnormality in their appearance, speech
or manner. Such continued investigation is the duty of every citizen
to his or her country and not merely a way of life for a journalist
or a special interest for a historian.

Chapter 4

On or Off the Record

Medical historians study and, if necessary, reshape their human targets. They are neither muck-rakers nor scandal-mongers for their approach is the same as papyrologists analysing ancient manuscripts or archaeologists carefully sorting out prehistoric remains or mosaics. Much of this painstaking reconstruction enhances and usually confirms what has long been known. Occasionally the accepted view of some ancient legend, of both individuals and civilizations, is challenged, sometime to the discomfort of the academic or conventional establishment.

New books dealing with legendary figures, although often excusably repetitive about actions and events long ago revealed, clearly cause discomfort to some reviewers who in turn cast doubt on the motives of the authors. Indeed, the review of one of two new books about President Kennedy which appeared in 1991 included a lay diagnosis of the motives which historians, presumably, including those medically qualified, are accused of harbouring; 'Reeves (the author) appears to be in his mid-fifties, a time of life when prurient curiosity about other people's sexual partners tends to be superseded by a morbid interest in their health'[1].

It may be morbid, it may even be prurient. But over forty-five years after President Roosevelt's death, and more than twenty years after his cardiologist had made available a detailed account of the last year of his life, interest in and curiosity about certain officially unexplained aspects of his medical history still persist.

The life and death of President Roosevelt is a continual reminder of how difficult it is to assess any relationship between pathological change and performance. Those who try are accused of speculation and of relying on second-hand unqualified sources and rumours. Roosevelt's triumph over his crippling poliomyelitis after 1921 may have persuaded him that any problem, personal or political, could be overcome.

For the first ten years of his presidency the main news was of his regular nasal wash-outs performed by his naval doctor, Ross McIntire, an ear, nose and throat specialist. These washouts had an unexpected side effect. They confused the German secret service. In June 1941 a report sent via the Pan-American clipper to Shanghai and relayed to Berlin stated that Roosevelt had uraemia. Washington gossip had been garbled and the sinus washouts had become bladder catheterization[2].

It was not until, or just after, the Teheran meeting of the 'big three' (Churchill, Roosevelt and Stalin) in November 1943 that there was cause for concern. In March 1944 Dr Howard Bruenn, a cardiologist and reserve officer in the US Navy Medical Corps, found that Roosevelt had a blood pressure of 186/100, left ventricular failure, slight cyanosis, acute bronchitis and breathlessness[3]. As far back as April 1937 his blood pressure was above average. At a time when there was no effective treatment his blood pressure increased until his death, despite short working days and long absences from the White House. In May 1944 a blood pressure of 240/130 mm Hg was noted by Bruenn, and on 12 April 1945, one of 300/190 as he lay dying of a massive cerebral haemorrhage. Blood pressure readings vary from day to day and Roosevelt's rose one evening in September 1944 just after watching a film about Woodrow Wilson.

In 1944 Roosevelt also had abdominal pain attributed to gall bladder stones, and lost appetite and weight. But McIntire told newsmen in September 1944 that Roosevelt's health was 'good, very good'. Daily contact can blur the signs of change. Colleagues, relatives and foreigners who only saw him at intervals were all shocked by his facial deterioration. The films taken at Yalta show a cadaveric figure puffing at a cigarette. Only the least bad photographs of Roosevelt at Yalta were released at the time. Lord Moran, Churchill's physician, wrote in his diary on 7 February 1945 that:

> 'the president appears a very sick man. He has all the symptoms of hardening of the arteries of the brain in an advanced stage, so I give him only a few months to live.'[4].

Moran can hardly be accused of being an observer who lacked medical skills. The view from inside the conference was even worse. Sir Alexander Cadogan, the senior and experienced official of the Foreign Office, wrote on 25 February:

> 'I got the impression that most of the time he hardly knew what it was all about. And whenever he was called on to preside over any meeting he failed to make any attempt to grip it or guide it, and sat generally speechless or, if he made any intervention, it was generally completely irrelevant'[5].

Physicians regret their past failures in diagnosis but they depend on current knowledge. In 1944 Roosevelt had hypertension and bronchitis. At that time these were considered separate conditions with one thing in common—there was no effective treatment. In 1986 Dr Bert Edward Park, a neurosurgeon and historian, argued that a combination of these conditions compounds disability[6]. In the twenty-five years since Roosevelt's death the respiratory physiologists have clarified the metabolic effects of chronic obstructive pulmonary disease, chronic heart failure, and the mental changes of secondary metabolic encephalopathy. These are confusion, lethargy, poor judgement and drowsiness. When Bruenn first examined Roosevelt in 1944 he already had heart failure and bronchitis with cyanosis and breathlessness at rest. He was a candidate for encephalopathy due to cerebral hypoxia and carbon dioxide retention. The signs and symptoms are intermittent. Does this explain why, at Quebec in 1944, and Yalta in 1945, Roosevelt sat vacant and remote with his mouth open?; and why at Yalta he was 'vague and loose and ineffective'? His physicians should not be blamed. Only now do we know that the transient unawareness or confusion of this encephalopathy may be caused by temporary worsening of heart or lung function.

Those who criticize the persistent curiosity about Roosevelt's incapacity could argue that the details given by Bruenn are sufficient to explain his rapid deterioration in 1944 and his death in April 1945 at the age of sixty-three. In reply, those whose curiosity still persists might ask, if this is the complete explanation, why the records at the Bethesda Naval Medical Center disappeared after his death. Between 1941 and 1945 Roosevelt went to Bethesda 29 times[14], using a variety of false names. It is admittedly difficult to prove a negative, but defenders of the accepted version of his illness could claim that there were no records in Bethesda, and none now in Hyde Park, because every detail had already been disclosed. As a result those who question whether Bruenn's account is complete can be smeared as rumour-mongers who rely on unfounded allegations based on misconceptions or failing memory.

In February 1970 Samuel M Day, an American surgeon, described a meeting with George Pack, a New York surgeon, in the course of which he related the following story. Dr Frank Lahey told Dr Pack that in the summer before the election for Roosevelt's fourth term the President came to Boston by special train to be examined by Dr Lahey at the Lahey Clinic. On completion of the examinations it was Dr Lahey's opinion that President Roosevelt had an advanced cancer of the stomach, apparently too far advanced for a surgical cure to be considered. Dr Lahey gave the President his diagnosis, told him he was gravely ill and should not run for a fourth term, and then added his solution; 'I suggest if you insist on running that you select a strong Vice-Presidential candidate to run with you'. With that Mr Roosevelt returned to Washington and 'as far as I know, nothing more was heard of his cancer'. Dr Pack wondered why Dr Lahey had never revealed it and stated that later he asked the doctor why he had not made this information public. Lahey replied that it was never to be revealed as long as any of the involved figures were still alive.

Day realized that his was 'a third-party story', he had 'absolutely no factual data to support it', and warned 'it has been so many years since our discussion (with Pack) that I could not swear it was a cancer of the stomach. It may have been some other organ, such as the lung, but I do not think so'[7].

Doctors are only too aware of gaps in memory and misperceptions. They are extremely cautious, to the exasperation of lawyers in court, about the evidence which they give, but their hesitation should not invariably cast doubt on its value. Two years later, in January 1972, Day wrote that he was not sure about the diagnosis of cancer which he had also mentioned to Kenneth Warren, chairman, department of surgery, Lahey Clinic, who stated that Roosevelt's problem was not cancer, 'but he did not clarify what it was'[8]. When approached later, Warren was 'intrigued' and suggested that the history of Roosevelt's illness should be pursued but 'through his family'[9]. In February 1972 Robert M Goldwyn, a Boston plastic and reconstructive surgeon, stated that he had learned from reliable sources that Dr Frank Lahey, described as Roosevelt's medical adviser during the war, had seen him for what was still rumoured to be a carcinoma of the prostate; 'there is absolutely no mention that this was a gastric carcinoma'[10].

In any profession it is essential to keep an open mind, and admit to the possibility of error, but Day's memory of events was accurate. In 1963 an American surgeon who has since made a unique study of Roosevelt, Harry S Goldsmith, also attended a lecture by Pack who stated that Lahey had told Roosevelt in 1944 'that he had a metastatic tumour and advised him not to run for a fourth term, since he would not survive this term of office if elected'. Lahey died in 1953 and Pack in 1969 but in 1975, when Goldsmith had the opportunity of examining Pack's papers, his diaries had been lost or misplaced and, although there were records of well-known individuals (presumably his own patients), there was no mention of Roosevelt.

As it was twelve years since Pack's lecture Goldsmith, like Day, 'began to question the accuracy of his own memory'. He found that some surgeons who were present at the 1963 lecture had remembered Pack's reference to Roosevelt while others had forgotten. One did recall Pack's statement that Roosevelt had a terminal malignant condition and confirmed that Pack had made the same point when he himself was the guest of Pack who was speaking on the same theme of 'Medicine and World History' at a medical dinner[11]. The validity of Lahey's statement to Pack cannot now be tested nor can another factor; both Lahey and Pack 'were notoriously rabid anti-Roosevelt men', according to William B Ober, an American pathologist and medical historian, who was a neighbour of both men at different times[12].

On 31 March 1944 there had been a group consultation of Roosevelt's medical advisers, including Frank Lahey who was an honorary medical consultant to the US Navy. In view of the patient's history of abdominal symptoms, which later became more severe, it is relevant that Bruenn wrote in 1970 that 'Dr Lahey was particularly interested in the gastrointestinal tract but submitted that no surgical procedure was indicated'. An alternative diagnosis and explanation was provided by the agents of the Federal Bureau of Investigation who, in October 1944, had begun to track down those in medical circles who were indulging in gossip about Roosevelt's ill-health. The FBI should also have checked with the Office of Strategic Services (OSS), the forerunner of the CIA, whose members had seen a Lahey Clinic report stating that the president would not survive another term[13]. At the end of November 1944, when Roosevelt had been re-elected for an unprecedented fourth term, J Edgar Hoover, the FBI director, reported the latest rumours circulating in Washington, allegedly from 'informed White House circles'.

Consequently it was widely claimed that William Calhoun (Pete) Stirling, a urological surgeon, had recently examined Roosevelt and, although surgery was indicated, declined to operate because of Roosevelt's poor condition. It was added that he did not wish to become known as the man who killed the president[14]. A sensible precaution since only nine years later a British surgeon was stigmatized as the man who cut Anthony Eden's common bile duct. The gossip hinted that Lahey when consulted confirmed that surgery was necessary and it would be performed after the election. The FBI report concluded that Lahey had insisted that Roosevelt be operated on at his clinic for commercial and advertising reasons. Again, in 1953 when one of his staff, Richard Cattell, was asked to examine Eden in London after the bungled operation, it was Lahey who insisted that Eden had to come to his Boston clinic for the surgical repair.

Historians prefer to rely on official and academic sources but even the bizarre should not be ignored and has to be taken into account. In January 1945 Roosevelt's birthday celebrations at the White House were unusual. He was not present as he was on his way to the Crimea for the Yalta conference. Mrs Roosevelt played hostess to a number of Hollywood guests, including contemporary stars such as Myrna Loy, Margaret O'Brien, Joe E Brown, Gene Kelly, Jane Wyman (Reagan's first wife), Danny Kaye, Alan Ladd, Victor Borge and Veronica Lake.

In Veronica Lake's memoirs written with Donald Bain and published in 1969, when she had settled in England, she stated that late on at the reception, and alone with Mrs Roosevelt, the latter suddenly blurted out 'the president has cancer of the prostate gland. He'll be operated on when he returns'. She had no idea why she had confined in Veronica Lake, whom she had no reason to choose, but asked her to treat her words as confidential. It seems improbable that Veronica Lake or Bain could have invented the precise diagnosis although critics of such an unlikely, even unreliable, source could argue that at best she was aware of the current Washington gossip and, later in life at worst, put words into Mrs Roosevelt's mouth[15].

Yet there is indirect evidence that Roosevelt's prostate could have been enlarged and was causing urinary obstruction and early renal impairment. Stanley P Reimann, an American pathologist, learned from one of his closest friends who had treated Roosevelt, that the president had chronic uraemia. It was also common knowledge, at the time of Roosevelt's fourth election in 1944, and possibly one of the rumours attracting FBI attention, that Roosevelt's blood urea was raised to 100 mg/dl. However, in Bruenn's account of Roosevelt's last year he makes no mention of Roosevelt's blood urea and wrote that 'at no time was there any evidence of renal dysfunction'[3].

Roosevelt's terminal illness could really be turned into a Perry Mason series; the case of the mysterious malignancy, the case of the President's prostate and, finally, the case of the missing mole. In May 1961 Francis M Massie, an American surgeon, wrote that he had thought since 1945 that Roosevelt had died of intracranial metastases from a malignant melanoma. Before 1943 his photographs showed a large pigmented naevus on his left eyebrow which presumably was removed since it was not visible after that year. He expanded on his theory by describing his experience at a meeting of the American Surgical Association in April 1949. Of a series of studies illustrating the radical treatment of malignant melanoma shown by a member of staff of the Walter Reed Hospital, only one lacked a serial number. It showed a gross section of a brain with a large metastatic melanoma in the right hemisphere and was dated 14 April 1945, the day on which Roosevelt's body arrived from Warm Springs, Georgia, where he had died on 12 April[16].

Goldsmith has studied photographs of Roosevelt from his early days at Groton and Harvard but considers that a pigmented lesion did not appear until 1932. It enlarged over the years but never appeared after November 1943 in any photograph which he had studied.

Alas, the ubiquitous Ober, who also assisted at Forrestal's autopsy at Bethesda, lays the melanotic ghost. In the summer of 1949 he was shown a slide of Roosevelt's skin lesion. It revealed seborrhoeic keratosis or, depending on terminology, inverted basal cell papilloma with a fair amount of melanin in the basal layer. In his view it was entirely benign[17].

In the published article, based on the lecture which Massie attended, the relevant brain specimen was labelled 'A-14-15'. Could this have had a meaning other than 14 and 15 April? There are no other illustrations to compare[18].

Forty years after Roosevelt's death what would be categorized by some as a morbid interest in his health still persisted, possibly because there had been no autopsy. In October 1985 it was reported that Goldsmith, in view of his long period of research into Roosevelt's health, was taking legal action to obtain a document described as the

Lahey memorandum. In two newspaper reports it was disclosed that in 1944 Lahey had examined Roosevelt and stated that he was in good health in contrast to later speculation by medical historians that he was unfit to run for a fourth term. When Lahey died in 1953 the memorandum was handed over to Linda M Strand, his business manager. She passed it in turn to her lawyers, Herrick and Smith, but when she gave her permission for Goldsmith to see the memorandum they refused to hand it over, while a lawyer for the Lahey Clinic objected to its release on the grounds that patients would ask 'what protection do you give us?' Lahey had instructed that details should only be released if there was posthumous criticism of his professional relationship with Roosevelt. Earlier in 1985 a judge had ruled that there was not enough evidence of criticism of Lahey to justify release of the document.

An attempt was also made by the National Archives and Record Administration to ensure the preservation of the memorandum as 'there had been substantial speculation that Dr Lahey in fact diagnosed the president as being gravely ill', that Lahey told another doctor that he had 'stomach cancer too advanced for a surgical cure' and had advised the president that 'he was too ill to seek re election'[19]. The Agency added that the memorandum 'should shed considerable light on the role of the human factor at a decisive stage in American history'[20]. One coincidence may have been irrelevant but James Roosevelt Jr, the president's grandson, was a partner in Herrick and Smith, the law firm witholding release of the memorandum.

On 18 February 1986 the Supreme Judicial Court for the Commonwealth of Massachusetts passed judgement in the case of Linda M Strand versus Herrick and Smith with others. A judgement was entered which required Herrick and Smith to deliver the Lahey memorandum to Strand. She passed the document to Goldsmith who understandably has not yet disclosed the contents. He wishes to include them in a book which he is preparing on this and other medical aspects of Roosevelt's last year. As yet no American publisher has expressed an interest in his proposal. One even pointed out that to those under forty years of age Roosevelt is as remote as Chester Arthur who was president from 1881 to 1885.

Even if all the medical details are available there is no certainty in life or death. The white-coated specialists who sit through the grand rounds at the Royal Postgraduate Medical School in London or the Massachusetts General Hospital may agree on a precise clinical and pathological diagnosis. They would not attempt to predict when or to what degree the possible effects of several pathological changes may first have influenced the patient's physical and mental capacity. The unhappy doctor in the witness box and the medical historian can neither prove nor be precise about cause or effect. Like the traditional jury, they can only reach a reasonable verdict after due and conscientious consideration of many factors of varying significance and reliability.

The career of Louis Alfred Johnson, the 250-lb American Secretary of Defense from 1949 to 1950, shows that even the comprehensive autopsy, carried out after his death in April 1966, can neither explain his reported eccentricity in office nor expunge the later diagnosis made by those without medical qualifications or knowledge. Johnson took office in March 1949, replacing James Forrestal who committed suicide in May. Johnson had decided that Forrestal was disturbed in the month before he resigned; his eyes bulged and he had the same symptoms that he had noted in his own daughter who had an incurable mental disorder. By March 1950 there were scenes in Johnson's office due to his reported outbursts of rage and in September President Truman asked for his resignation.

In 1970, four years after Johnson's death, Dean Acheson, who had been Truman's Secretary of State, wrote of Johnson, 'His conduct became too outrageous to be explained by mere cussedness. It did not surprise me when some years later he underwent a brain operation'. Acheson continued; 'Johnson's behaviour passed beyond the peculiar to the impossible. I have already stated my belief that this was the result of a brain malady, which ultimately proved fatal'[21].

General Omar N Bradley, then Chief of Staff, US Army, complained of Johnson's egotistical drive to run the whole government and quotes what Truman wrote about him in his private diary; 'I am of the opinion that Potomac fever, and a *pathological condition* are to blame'[22]. Referring also to Forrestal, whom Johnson had succeeded, Bradley added that 'unwittingly Truman had replaced one mental case with another'.

Johnson lived until April 1966 when it was reported that he had died after a series of strokes. Autopsy reports are made available in America and one of five pages was obtained by John Nichols, himself a pathologist. Johnson's terminal admission to the Washington Hospital Center was because of generalized and sudden convulsions and bilateral lower lobe pneumonia. The immediate cause of death was acute purulent tracheobronchitis with chronic brain syndrome as a contributing factor. His first admission, 13 months before his death, was for paroxysms of atrial flutter and mental derangement. Presumably on this occasion he underwent further treatment because in another section of the report it is stated that 'thirteen months prior to terminal admission (he) had had a craniotomy for evacuation of a subdural haematoma'.

Examination of the skull and brain revealed the left craniotomy site and old, healing cystic infarcts in the occipital lobe of the right cerebral hemisphere which was softer than the rest of the brain. One cystic infarct communicated with the subarachnoid space through a hole in the cortex. There was marked, generalized atherosclerosis with recent mural thrombi in both common iliac arteries. Microscopy of the cystic areas showed infarcts with marginal areas of gliosis together with foam cells and pigment-laden macrophages.

Acheson or his research assistants may well have heard garbled reports about Johnson's mental state in 1966 and, without justification, back-dated its presumed effects by some sixteen years. It is impossible to determine how long the cerebral changes and, in particular, the subdural haematoma, had been present. Bradley's autobiography with its accusations was not published until 1983, seventeen years after Johnson's death.

Free access to medical records can remove unjustifiable accusations. When he took over the Department of Defense in 1949 Johnson had the unenviable task of completing the unification of the Navy, Air Force and Marines. His removal of the Navy from its strategic air mission and cancellation of an aircraft carrier led to the resignation of the Navy Secretary. His approval of the purchase of B-36 bombers was criticized as a 'billion dollar blunder'. It was hoped to improve the capacity for long-range inter-continental strikes despite unjustified rumours that the B-36 was inefficient and its procurement involved dubious political and commercial deals. In September 1949 a letter of complaint, signed by several admirals, maintained that unification had not been achieved and that, as a result, morale in the US Navy was low. Johnson may also have inflamed his critics by opposing Acheson's policies in the Far East. He had virtually lied to Truman, however, by the underhand manner in which he arranged for the president to approve Gordon Gray as Army Secretary. As Truman concluded, 'the terrible thing about all this is that Johnson doesn't realize he has done anything wrong'[23].

There was seemingly nothing wrong with Johnson's mental capacity over the next few years. He returned to his law firm, became president of General Dyestuffs Corporation, a director of Consolidated Vultee Aircraft Corporation and, in Clarksburg, West Virginia, of the Union National Bank and the Community Savings and Loan Company.

The understandable inter-service wrangling had unhinged Forrestal despite his long service in governmental departments. The battle for money and prestige, particularly bitter between the branches of the armed forces, is familiar to those in any branch of administration. If Louis Johnson's behaviour appeared irrational to those who were not receiving the appropriations to which they believed themselves entitled, it was improper and unjustified years after the event to 'diagnose' a cerebral tumour.

The records of an autopsy do not answer all historical questions. Those of medical practitioners, written often in haste so that their content is not a complete record, may not be any more revealing. Indeed these records may not be the only ones available. Patients discuss their illnesses with many individuals outside the profession.

These discussions are remembered with varying degrees of accuracy and are repeated in diaries or biographies and also passed to third parties who in turn may later circulate the information. These snippets of information should first be examined and then retained or rejected by every type of historian, but should not be dismissed as idle talk or tittle tattle without due consideration.

The details of Louis Johnson's autopsy should prevent any conclusions being dismissed, to quote Joyce Carol Oates, as 'pathography'. In his review of a book on Katharine Graham, Arthur Schlesinger, Jr, entitled it 'The Perils of Pathography' and quoted Joyce Carol Oates' definition; biographies that revel in 'dysfunction and disaster, illnesses and pratfalls, failed marriages and failed careers, alcoholism and breakdowns and outrageous conduct'[24]. Incidentally, Schlesinger cites Crispell and Gomez[14] as producers of pathography when they state that Roosevelt visited the Naval Medical Center at Bethesda twenty-nine times between 1941 and 1945. Schlesinger claims that the visits were not attendances but occasions when specimens were sent to the laboratory for analysis. Crispell and Gomez have data to prove that they are correct. The charge of publishing pathography cannot be levelled at the cardiologist who treated an American general, and was concerned about putting the record, and, understandably, his own correct diagnosis straight.

When the health of those in public or official positions is questioned there is a case for relaxing the rules about absolute confidentiality in order to put the record straight. There are occasions when a doctor may wish to break the rule about confidentiality, not only to correct the record for academic or historical reasons but, equally important, to defend his reputation. In his autobiography published in 1956 General Matthew B Ridgway, who led the US Army in the Korean War, became supreme commander in the Far East and Europe and was finally chief of staff US Army, described a sudden illness in Trieste harbour in September 1945. First he had blurred vision, remembers lying weak and ill but still conscious on the deck of a launch and then after a black-out recovering consciousness in a British field hospital.

Ridgway stated that he was seen by Dr Dupuy, later a cardiologist in New Orleans, but refused his advice to retire and demanded to return to full duty. He maintained that other doctors could find no abnormality and attributed the black-out to a 'capillary burst'. When approached out of curiosity in 1978 Dupuy gave an entirely different version of the incident[25]. Ridgway had a sudden attack of loss of consciousness during which he collapsed, bit his tongue and had muscular twitching. There was a past history of a previous black-out and the provisional diagnosis was of syncope or possibly epilepsy.

Subsequently Ridgway apologized for his incorrect account to Dupuy who was still concerned about the description and the effect on his personal reputation. He did not consider the question of professional confidentiality, only that the events be reported to protect his professional standing. Serial electrocardiograms had revealed no abnormality and the final diagnosis lay between epilepsy, syncope, petit mal or carotid sinus syncope. Dupuy had discussed the possibility of more extensive investigations to exclude a cerebral tumour. Facilities were not available in Italy and such an examination elsewhere might come to the attention of the Surgeon General's office. Ridgway ruled this out and Dupuy accepted full responsibility. He packed all Ridgway's medical records into his personal kit and only the inaccurate statements in the autobiography compelled him to give an accurate account and defend his action.

In this case a cardiologist's correct diagnosis of a neurological condition was triumphantly vindicated. General Ridgway died on 27 July 1993 at the age of ninety-eight, an unlikely outcome had he actually experienced a myocardial infarction as early as 1945. Whether General Ridgway and physicians other than Dupuy considered that, to the US Army, a minor 'cardiac episode' from which he recovered was a more publicly acceptable diagnosis than a minor fit can always be debated. There certainly seems no need to suppress or distort the evidence.

Chapter 5

Brain Failure

Memorial lectures tend to be conventional with dutiful members of the establishment and, if available, a representative descendant listening with studied attention. An unconventional and stimulating note was struck at the 17th Victor Horsley memorial lecture at University College Hospital, London, in November 1978[1]. Its subject and title were unusual, even provocative, and it was only the distinction of the lecturer, Dr William Gooddy, that permitted a controversial theme to be discussed and later published. His title, 'Brain Failure in Private and Public Life', would have been excluded as too provocative or even unscientific if suggested by the average speaker. 'Brain failure' was, and still is, not accepted medical jargon, whilst hinting that even unnamed individuals in public life could have such a condition verged on impiety besides breaking the rules on medical secrecy.

Gooddy explained that the idea of the failing brain came to him around 1940 and he had first spoken on brain failure at University College Hospital twenty-five years before. To those in the audience who regularly spoke of heart, liver and renal failure it may have seemed surprising that the term was not already widely used. Not that Gooddy claimed originality, because earlier in 1978 he had found a monograph by Horsley and Sturge written in 1907 on *Alcohol in the Human Body* in which the authors pointed out that a large dose at one sitting caused first exhilaration and then brain failure and collapse. Discovery and revelation often come in pairs leading to endless discussion and argument about priority. Was it another pioneer, or a pupil of Gooddy's, who wrote the anonymous editorial on brain failure in the *Journal of the Royal College of General Practitioners* for August 1977, over a year before the Victor Horsley Lecture?

Gooddy's guide to the symptoms and signs of brain failure should be available to every politician, journalist, selection board, shareholder, voter and taxpayer. What he describes as intermittent symptoms can be disturbing to the introspective as they do occur in the young and middle-aged as well as in the ageing; uncertainty, instability, loss of concentration, occasional odd behaviour, changes of mood and incompetence. More important and diagnostic are loss of memory, failing concentration, loss of speech fluency, poverty of abstract thinking, failure of judgement, insight and behaviour, loss of factual knowledge and words, aggression, paranoid delusions or hallucinations and suicidal depression.

47

Clinicians select extreme examples of physical and mental disease to demonstrate to students or on 'grand rounds', as the symptoms and signs can more easily and unforgettably be demonstrated. For such reasons it is convenient to discuss brain failure in two aged leaders, one of whom did not retire until his 81st year whilst the other was constitutionally bound to leave office after the maximum two terms when he was just short of his seventy-eighth birthday.

Through his varied achievements, vivid speeches and the image of supreme command which he projected, Churchill became a populist leader in Britain's darkest hour, eternally idolized by the majority and criticized by few. Tiring perhaps of my repeated references to the pathology of leadership one critic wrote that if Churchill had failed my fitness tests in 1940 I would not have been around forty years later to write about him. Other leaders might have been better or worse and could also have shown some or all the signs of brain failure shown by Churchill. Despite his outward reverence of democracy and parliamentary government Robert Menzies, serving his first term of office as Australian prime minister, commented on Churchill's autocratic rule. After a visit to London in April 1941 he observed that the British War Cabinet was 'deplorable—dumb men most of whom disagree with Winston but none of whom dare to say so . . . the Chiefs of Staff are without exception Yes-men, and a politician runs the Services. Winston is a dictator. . . . The people have set him up as little less than God, and his power is therefore terrific'[2].

The perception of close colleagues and their shrewd observations about Churchill, though couched in lay terms, paints a clinical picture of brain failure as early as 1942 in his sixty-eighth year. Particular attention must be paid to the diaries of Leo Amery published only in 1988, since he had been at school at Harrow with Churchill who sent him to the India Office in 1940 after lifelong political association.

On 26 February 1942 Amery noted at a meeting of the India Committee that Winston shows 'complete inability to grasp even the most elementary point' leading him to feel for the first time that 'not merely he is unbusinesslike but that he is over-tired and really losing his grip altogether'; a stranger would consider him 'a rather amusing but quite gaga old gentleman who could not understand what people were talking about'[3]. In March 1944 the then General Sir Alan Brooke, Chief of the Imperial General Staff, thought Churchill was 'losing ground rapidly' and seemed 'incapable of concentrating for a few minutes on end, and keeps wandering continuously'[4]. On 3 April Amery remarked that it was no wonder that Churchill looked so tired after a three-hour cabinet meeting; 'Government by monologue is a pretty exhausting affair'[3]. In the same month Sir Alexander Cadogan, permanent under-secretary at the Foreign Office noted in his diary that Churchill was breaking down as 'he rambles without a pause', and on 17 July that he was ageing and 'the rambling talk is *frightful*'[5]. On 7 August 1944 after a day with Churchill in Normandy, Churchill struck the then General Montgomery as old, tired, restless and unable to concentrate or make a decision.

By November 1944 Churchill's behaviour gave grounds for even more concern. Amery wrote that Churchill 'has only indulged in wild and indeed hardly sane tirades in Cabinet'[3], that he never reads papers or seeks opinions so that the point of any discussion is lost.

Even his faithful inner circle were expressing similar concern about 'The Boss'. Churchill's dispatch box was in an appalling muddle with many outstanding documents requiring a decision. He wasted time and was unable, unwilling or too tired to deal with demanding problems. In January 1945 Clement Attlee, deputy prime minister, complained to Churchill about his unmethodical approach to cabinet business which was harming the war effort. He had to point out to Churchill that it was 'very exceptional' for him to have read the cabinet agenda and papers so half an hour was spent in explaining what could have been understood in a few minutes' reading[5]. A damning verdict came from his loyal private secretary, John Colville, in April and May 1945; Churchill 'is now becoming an administrative bottleneck' and 'there is a voluminous weight of paper which awaits his attention'[6].

Churchill's brain failure became obvious to his inner circle and, increasingly to cabinet and parliamentary colleagues, during his second premiership between November 1951 and April 1955. Lord Moran, his personal physician, wrote a virtual day-by-day account of his sad decline which still makes distressing reading. Churchill's family regard Moran as a hostile witness and claim with some reason that he was only summoned when the patient was ill, and did not see him in the course of his continuing and productive contributions to his high office. Bemused by the exotic and romantic image which had long been projected, an image that many wanted to perpetuate, any suggestion that the idol had feet of clay was dismissed with disbelief and even hostility.

Yet Moran's meticulous notes bring the readers back from fantasy and near mythology to stark reality. In August 1949 Churchill had his first stroke described as 'cramp' in the right arm and leg, and a second minor one in February 1952 when cerebral arterial spasm caused dysphasia. On 23 June 1953 at a banquet for the Italian prime minister he had his third and most serious stroke when he could not rise from his chair at the dinner table and had difficulty with his speech. Next morning Moran found that the left side of his mouth sagged and he was unsteady on the feet and by 27 June there was a loss of power in the left hand with dragging and weakness of the left leg. Lord Brain gave a gloomy neurological prognosis and on

25 August doubted whether Churchill would be able to make public speeches or answer questions in the House of Commons.

Like many other patients Churchill defied his doctors despite the increasing signs of brain failure and the three strokes indicative of the exacerbation of his intellectual incapacity due to cerebral arteriosclerosis and thrombosis. Early into his second term on 26 January 1952 Moran noted that 'the old appetite for work had gone; everything had become an effort'[7], a view echoed by John Colville who said that Churchill was not working properly and that five sheets of documents had to be concentrated into one paragraph. It is not disclosed what tablets were prescribed for Churchill before he spoke at the Conservative Party conference and answered parliamentary questions in October and made the first speech following the stroke in the House of Commons in November. Whether these were amphetamine, then fashionable and acceptable, or placebos fortified by confidence engendered by Moran is not known. Churchill continued to rely on them before international meetings, as at Bermuda in December 1953, and even for cabinet meetings.

By 1954 his brain failure should have been apparent to the world but, if it was, there was little adverse comment. He spoke badly in the House of Commons in February and also at the Conservative party conference in October when he fumbled for words, said sovereignty instead of solvency and 1850 instead of 1950, but told Moran that his pill was wonderful. At a time when he was hoping to arrange talks with the Russians he made a serious mistake in a constituency speech in November 1954. He claimed that before the end of the war in North-West Europe he had ordered Montgomery to collect discarded German weapons which could be re-issued to them if the Russian advance continued beyond the agreed boundaries. As the telegram to Montgomery could not be traced, Churchill had to issue a humiliating apology to parliament and confess that he had not checked on the alleged message.

Churchill's most loyal defender, his son Randolph, countered what he regarded as unjustified slurs on his father's performance by citing his activities in parliament between his 80th birthday on 30 November 1954 and his retirement on 5 April 1955. In the thirteen weeks when parliament was sitting Churchill participated in three major debates and gave one hundred and three answers to one hundred and twenty-two questions besides dealing with a hundred and eighty-three supplementary questions on twenty-three days.

No doubt like most political performers he could rise to the occasion but behind the scenes his inner circle had been concerned. In May 1952 Colville noted that Churchill's low periods had increased and his concentration was impaired. In November of the same year he was tired and visibly ageing, found it hard to compose a speech and ideas no longer flowed while, so far as the public show was concerned, he made two 'strangely simple' errors in the House of Commons. Yet he composed every word of two speeches in the House on defence and foreign affairs as late as March 1955. The ageing brain works in fits and starts. The contemporary televised proceedings of parliament give an opportunity for commentators and historians to study the members both when they are standing to speak or attract attention, and possibly even more revealing, when they are slumped in their seats and unaware that they are still on stage and in the public view.

President Reagan was nearly seventy when he began what was to be an eight-year term in January 1981 during which he had to undergo several surgical procedures. These included a near-fatal gun shot wound of his chest in March 1981, an extensive colonic resection in July 1985, a prostatectomy in 1987, and in both these years, minor surgery for removal of basal cell carcinomata on his nose. Although on these occasions he received sympathy and understanding from the American people there were no illusions about his methods of work, extensive leisure and mental capacity.

As early in his presidential term as September 1981 flippant columnists were poking fun at his leisurely schedule and apparent indifference to urgent affairs of state. Lewis Grizzard[8] described his schedule as '8 am presidential wakeup call, 9 am second presidential wakeup call and 9.30 am Ed Meese goes to presidential bedroom and tickles president's feet so he will get up'. Next at 10.30 am briefing with National Security Council, 10.32 am end briefing, 11 to 11.30 am meeting when Rep. What's-his-face from Texas explains to president what synthetic fuels programme is all about while between 11.30 and 11.31 the president responds by asking Rep. What's-his-face from Texas about Cowboys' chances in coming football season'.

Art Buchwald put words into Reagan's mouth[9]; 'I went to California and had a great time. I went horseback riding and slept late and worked on the farm and fed the cattle, and fired fourteen thousand air traffic controllers'. David Stockman told him to cut the budget by $40 billion, 'Cap' Weinberger said he would need another $4 billion for a new ABM system to protect our MX missiles, so 'I told him not to worry and he and David should work it out because the veterinarian was coming at two to look at one of my horses'. Buchwald's satirical page concludes with the words; 'Nancy and I are talking about coming back next year for three months because now that I'm president I have a lot more time on my hands'.

These two facetious articles were not far removed from actual events. Lou Cannon who had followed Reagan's career wrote that during his presidency he had spent more time watching films than any other activity. He spent one hundred and eighty-three week-ends at the Camp David retreat during his eight years as president, usually watching two films on each occasion, and a total of three hundred and forty-five days at his 688-acre Rancho del Cielo in

California[10]. He was also closely studied by Simon Hoggart, the contemporary correspondent of *The Observer* in Washington, who noted that the Reagans were in their pyjamas by 6.00 pm and may spend half their time in night attire. More serious is his observation that although Reagan spends much time asleep 'his waking hours are just as dreamy. Nothing is what it seems. The past is the present. Friends become enemies and vice-versa. Once solid certainties flicker, disappear and are forgotten'[11]. There is an uncomfortable analogy between Reagan's time-consuming preoccupation with films and Churchill's absorption with bezique and novels, linking their mutual indifference to state papers.

Perhaps some allowance can be made for Reagan's performance after an economic summit at Ottawa in 1981 as it was only four months after the attempt on his life. Cannon was later to write that Reagan 'was exhausted nearly to the point of incoherence throughout much of the interview and could not remember the substance of any subject that had been discussed apart from Mitterand's expression of anti-communism'. His speech was halting and he 'simply was unable to recall the contents of the talks in which he had just participated'[10].

After 1981 the after-effects of his chest wound could no longer excuse or explain his behavioural lapses. When in Brazil on a Latin American visit in 1982 he toasted the citizens of Bolivia. Economic summits, understandably perhaps, dealt with technical matters beyond his range of interest and knowledge but at an interview before the one held in Williamsburg in 1983 he was muddled as to exactly who the contestants were in the various Central American states[12]. Busy men and women, who are forced to meet new and old acquaintances by day and night, may not unreasonably confuse names and faces. The man whom Gore Vidal called The Acting President had already begun to fluff his lines.

Art Buchwald's column about David Stockman and Casper Weinberger trying to persuade Reagan about the defence budget must not be dismissed as satirical humour. Weinberger knew how to impress Reagan and influence his decisions and appeared at an actual meeting with a puppet show of three soldiers; a pigmy without a rifle representing the former President Carter's budget, a four-eyed wimp with a tiny rifle representing the $1.33 trillion budget suggested by David Stockman and GI Joe with helmet, flak jacket and M-60 machine gun representing the $1.46 trillion budget favoured by Weinberger. Needless to say his 'visuals' swayed the president to agree to his larger budget[13].

Old men forget but they remember and continue to believe the legends which subconsciously they have fabricated. In 1983 Reagan told Yitzhak Shamir that as an army photographer he had taken pictures of the death camps although he had never served in Europe. In actual fact he made training films for pilots, wore US Air Force uniform but never saw any action, and refused to fly again after a short but turbulent flight from Los Angeles to Catalina[14].

By 1987 Reagan was showing signs of his 76 years so that 'his memory lapses and rambling discourses are no longer a source of friendly jokes, but one of concern'[12]. A foreign diplomat who had recently met senior Western officials at an economic summit in Venice said that he was distracted 'as if he had his mind on something else', whilst another remarked on his physical and mental fatigue[12].

As a British reporter, Simon Hoggart could be emotionally independent but he looked back on 1987 as 'a year of sleepy, hollow Ron', where 'fact and fiction have become blurred, where reality is a pale shadow of its TV image, where the trivial is recalled with clarity and the important is forgotten'. Between November 1986 and March 1987 Reagan gave six different opinions about arms deals with Iran to rescue the hostages; 'it was not a mistake', 'I didn't make a mistake', 'I do not think it was a mistake', 'mistakes were made', 'serious mistakes were made', and 'it was a mistake'. In October 1987 his personal and intellectual prestige fell to its lowest level when at his first press conference for seven months he was asked if he would be willing to raise taxes;

> 'But the problem is the—the deficit is—or should I say— wait a minute, the spending, I should say, of gross national product, forgive me—the spending is roughly 23 to 24 per cent. So that it is in—it what is increasing, while the revenues are staying proportionately the same and what would be the proper amount they should, that we should be taking from the private sector'[15].

Reagan through his acting experience presented such an engaging image that blunders due to thoughtlessness or ignorance were forgiven and forgotten. On 11 August 1984 while checking sound for a regular radio talk from his California ranch Reagan joked; 'My fellow Americans, I am pleased to tell you I have signed legislation to outlaw Russia forever. We begin bombing in five minutes'[16]. The 'broadcast' went out live, leading the Russians to say he was a warmonger and the Democrats that he was irresponsible. He would not have been human if he had remembered the names of thousands of faces who had brief moments on stage at the White House. When he shook Denis Healey's hand in 1987 and said 'nice to meet you Mr Ambassador', the actual ambassador said later that he had already met the president eleven times. Some of Reagan's errors must have caused pain and even offence to fellow Americans. On the same visit Healey was told that Reagan had mistaken General Colin Powell, born in Jamaica and then acting as deputy to the National Security adviser, for a janitor[17].

Lou Cannon, the White House correspondent of *The Washington Post*, is not only an experienced reporter but had the inestimable advantage, denied to physicians and psychologists, of being able to study Reagan for many years at press conferences and interviews. In his opinion Reagan not only had a bad memory for names but one which was impaired by considerable gaps and also noticeably selective which resulted in irrelevant comments about past films and anecdotes. This was obvious in 1962 when Reagan, then aged only fifty-one, was required to give evidence when the Justice Department investigated his former employer, The Music Corporation of America. When pressed Reagan's reaction 'was to retreat toward constantly expanding areas of forgetfulness'[14]. After he became Governor of California on 1 January 1967 his aides remarked that 'he often did not remember what he had done, and sometimes not even what he had said'.

Twenty years later, and anticipating a further surgical procedure, President Reagan was due to be questioned by the Tower Commission. Donald Regan and two White House aides did their best on 3 January 1987 'to stimulate a presidential memory' about this first arms shipment in August 1985 which Reagan at first could not remember but McFarlane claimed he had approved. Two days later, on 5 January 1987 President Reagan underwent a transurethral resection of his prostate. Three weeks after surgery, on 26 January he admitted to the Commission, convened to investigate the rumours of the Irangate scandals, that he had authorized an arms shipment to Iran via the Israelis in August 1985 but denied any knowledge of the role of his National Security staff in helping the Nicaraguan contras and diverting funds from the Iran arms deal for their use. Robert McFarlane, who also gave evidence before the Tower board, wrote a letter to the House and Senate Intelligence Committees apologizing for Saudi Arabian contributions to the Contras, and then on 7 February swallowed at least twenty valium tablets.

The briefing which Reagan received on 3 January must have confused him. On 11 February he read out to the Commission the staff memo and claimed surprise about the arms shipment via Israel. He also included the background instructions provided by his staff on how best to present the evidence.

John Tower, Edward Muskie and Brent Scowcroft of the Commission never conceived that Reagan would be 'devoid of any independent recollection' or 'so mentally confused' and concluded that further questioning would be useless. In a letter to John Tower dated 20 February 1987 Reagan wrote 'I don't remember, period' and 'I am afraid that I let myself be influenced by others' recollections, not my own'. Scowcroft conceded that Reagan may have been informed of the arms deal with Israel and Iran 'in a way that never really registered' and 'unknowingly approved the diversion'. Although in a speech to the American people on 4 March he accepted responsibility for the arms trade he 'never completely admitted his complicity'[10].

As the Reagan act was drawing to its close his press conference at the end of the Moscow Summit on 1 June 1988 was disconcerting even to Americans. Of thirty-one questions accepted by Reagan or his minders, only one was from a Russian. Although only ten Russian journalists had been invited there were empty chairs because many reporters, some from the White House press corps, were absent as Gorbachev's concurrent meeting drew a bigger gate. Reagan gave 'one of his worst performances in recent times' and 'there were embarrassing pauses as he struggled for the right word'[18].

Reagan's struggle for the right word was more than an embarrassment for him and the reporters. As far back as 1984 it had led to an analysis of his mental state, and an evaluation of his increasing brain failure[19]. The study was carried out, not by foreign intelligence services or government, but by a British academic in London. Its author was a psychologist, Brian Butterworth of University College, London, whose research has been devoted to speech and its disturbances in normal individuals and those with brain damage. From 1979 to 1983 he was editor-in-chief of the journal *Linguistics* and a founding editor of *Language* and *Cognitive Processes*.

In view of the alleged deterioration of Reagan's speech patterns already noted in 1984, Butterworth decided to tape and evaluate his television debates with President Carter in 1980 and with Walter Mondale in 1984. He used five methods of comparison by assessing paragrammatisms, involving confusion in the use and order of words and grammatical forms, with omissions or additions and the use of singular verbs with plural nouns; slips of the tongue when the wrong word is chosen and parts of words are left out, disordered or incorrect; much longer pauses than usual; grammatical speech representing confused thought; and words per minute which show if the speaker is taking longer to express an opinion.

Butterworth's findings were revealing[20]. In the 1980 debate with Carter, Reagan's answers were clear and his sentences well formed, understandable and, if necessary, corrected. Four years later Reagen's replies had more grave errors and at times were so muddled that they could not be understood. The differences in Reagan's performance in the 1980 and 1984 debates could be measured. There were no paragrammatic errors in the Carter debate but an average of one every two hundred and twenty words in the first Mondale debate, and one every two hundred and ninety words in the second. Long pauses occurred less than once in a thousand words in 1980 but occurred five times more often in 1984 when there was also a nine per cent slowing of speech. The latter may be due to slowing of cerebration or a longer search for words and ideas.

What Butterworth regarded as the most significant change in 1984 compared with 1980 were what he described as confusional errors where the content of a sentence is seriously wrong and cannot be corrected, unlike a slip of the tongue which can be corrected or the whole sentence reworded. As far back as 1984 Butterworth's psychological diagnosis was forbidding. In the absence of formal medical and psychological tests the comparison of the 1980 and 1984 debates showed a decline in Reagan's intellectual capacity. Butterworth pointed out in 1984 that degeneration of the aged brain once started can lead to dementia in two years, and in 1987 was quoted as saying that Reagan had early senile dementia. Journalists and politicians would not dare to use the word but their varied observations would bear out Butterworth's prognosis*.

The gradual and inevitable mental deterioration of age can be balanced by knowledge gained, and at least partly ameliorated by experience, together with the support of devoted staff and colleagues. Little can offset the sudden and possibly permanent loss of function caused by a cerebral haemorrhage, tumour or trauma. John Davies, a former managing director of Shell Mex and BP, and later director of the Confederation of British Industry, was admirably qualified for advancement in what was hoped to be Edward Heath's reforms after 1970. Elected to parliament as member for Knutsford in June 1970, within six weeks as a consequence of the death of Iain Macleod, then Chancellor of the Exchequer, and a cabinet reshuffle, he was invited to join the cabinet as minister of technology in the newly formed Department of Trade and Industry. In 1972 as Chancellor of the Duchy of Lancaster he became responsible for European affairs.

At the Conservative Party Conference at Brighton in October 1978 John Davies made a calamitous speech during a debate on Rhodesia. It was later revealed that he had been ill for weeks with what were described as neuralgia and sinus trouble, and was feeling unwell on the day of the debate at the end of which he left to see a specialist. He was admitted to hospital for brain surgery and resigned his seat in November. He was found to have a brain tumour which, despite treatment, continued to grow until his death in July 1979. It is difficult to determine when the presence of such tumours first affect a patient's behaviour. A bizarre incident during the Christmas holiday of 1973 may have been unrelated to the brain tumour which was diagnosed much later. He warned his family of the evils that lay ahead and 'it was the last Christmas of its kind that we should enjoy'[21]. The fears that he expressed were shared by the 'higher level' of the armed forces and intelligence services, and may have been exacerbated by an explosion in his Fulham flat in 1972 caused by Angry Brigade terrorists.

The physical collapse of William Joseph Casey in December 1986 was as sudden as that of John Davies. It is described with clinical precision by his biographer, Joseph Persico[22]. After playing a major part in organizing Reagan's election campaign Casey was made Director of Central Intelligence in January 1981, three months short

---

*In November 1994 Ronald Reagan stated he had Alzheimer's disease which had been diagnosed the year before.

of his sixty-eighth birthday. His influence was considerable as he was not confined to CIA headquarters in Langley, Virginia just twelve miles from the White House. He was a member of Reagan's cabinet and also of the exclusive National Security Council and National Security Planning Group.

The CIA doctors were continually checking his blood pressure, literally at his desk as he continued phoning and reading. His blood pressure was recorded as around 160/105 and his compliance with treatment was spasmodic. In the summer of 1985 he was found to have a carcinoma of the prostate and, since a choice was offered, he selected radiation. In October 1986 an MRI examination revealed no evidence of spread. In November 1986, when Casey took part in secret visits to CIA agents in El Salvador, Costa Rica, Honduras and Nicaragua, he was obviously tired and dozed during meetings.

After 1 December he noticeably deteriorated. His aides noticed that his right hand was trembling and, appearing at long sessions of the Home Defence Appropriations Sub-committee, he was vulnerable to questioning and confused. On the 11 December on his way from Washington to Philadelphia for a memorial dinner he walked into an airport baggage cart, did not stand for the invocation at the dinner, and one foot dragged. On the plane back to Washington Richard Helms, a former Director of Central Intelligence, noticed that Casey held his glass at a precarious angle and spilled the contents and also, on getting off the plane, walked straight into the hatchway and hit his head. On 14 December he phoned a Washington newspaper correspondent three times about the same item within minutes. Next day, after the doctor had completed a routine blood pressure test in the director's office, Casey's speech failed and his right arm and leg started to jerk so violently that he nearly fell from his chair. After admission to Georgetown University Hospital a CAT scan revealed a mass on the left side of his brain. Surgery revealed this to be a lymphoma and, after a virtually speechless and paralysed Casey had resigned from the CIA in January 1987, he died of pneumonia in May.

Those in medical and surgical charge of Casey thought that, in view of the usual rate of growth and spread of lymphomas, Casey could have first been affected in September or October 1986. This would explain his fatigue on his trip to Central America, his poor performance in congressional hearings and, for the first time, lying during the proceedings, so different from his previous habit of evasion, omission and vagueness. The reported onset in the autumn of 1986 does not therefore absolve Casey from decisions, well before this date, to advocate the Iran arms deal, conceal the details from Congress and continue the war in Nicaragua despite Representative Boland's amendment barring any action to overthrow that country.

Professor William B Shapiro, of the Memorial Sloan-Kettering Cancer Center, New York, described how lymphomas grow like a network rather than in a mass, and that there are therefore regular and hard to define alterations in manner and cerebration which are missed or put down to stress. Several commentators have suggested that such changes might have started as early as 1985, rather than the autumn of 1986[23].

It is clear that for weeks, months, or years, depending on how the neuropathology is assessed, any discussions between the president and his director of central intelligence were influenced by their failing brains. Confusion was first confounded by Casey's diction which would be worthy of investigation by Brian Butterworth. Casey's speech had always been slurred, he pronounced Nicaragua as Nicawawa, 'he invariably mumbled softly, and no one knew if he was informing them or deceiving them'. As one aide said 'even if he told us what he was thinking we couldn't understand what he said'[24]. It is not surprising that he was called Mumbling Bill.

Unfortunately this also applied to Reagan whose understanding was further hampered by his partial deafness, and who said that you can ask a person to repeat himself twice but a third request seems rude; 'so I'd just nod my head, but I didn't know what he was actually saying'[22]. In this way dirty tricks can apparently receive the consent of the head of state who, when held to account in the future, can escape responsibility by the plausible denial that he knew anything of the plan.

It is appropriate that Dr William Gooddy should have the last word on brain failure as it is a state of mind which he has so vividly and clinically delineated. In an article sub-titled 'After Guinness' a leading medical journalist and investigator, Christine Doyle, commented on the return to City life in 1992 of the former Guinness chairman, Ernest Saunders[25]. In 1990, at the age of 55, he had been found guilty of an illegal share support operation during an abortive takeover bid for Distillers. Sentenced to serve five years' imprisonment it became common knowledge that a diagnosis of pre-senile dementia had been made.

At the Court of Appeal in 1991 the five-year sentence on Saunders was halved and after 10 months at Ford open prison he reappeared apparently fit and well*. During the appeal court proceedings four medical consultants gave evidence after examining Saunders and passed an opinion on his abnormal brain scan. Dr George Perkin, a Charing Cross Hospital neurologist, did not discount the abnormal brain scan but was not prepared to make a diagnosis of pre-senile dementia on this evidence alone, and without detailed psychological testing. Dr Patrick Gallwey, a forensic psychiatrist, stated that, since he had first seen Saunders in 1988, there were signs of what he called organic degeneration, while Dr Owen Lloyd, medical officer at Ford open prison, found Saunders slower, older than his true age and repetitive.

---

*Saunders' case has been referred back to the Court of Appeal in the light of new evidence which may lead to his aquittal.

Dr William Gooddy admitted that Saunders' brain scans revealed abnormality and, avoiding obscure terminology, concluded that there was less brain than would be expected in a person of his age; particularly in those areas necessary for judgement, decision and foresight. He hesitated to make a final diagnosis on one set of scans but, even without them, considered that Saunders showed signs of pre-senile dementia.

As a neurologist, and not a psychiatrist, Gooddy questioned whether the recent and obvious vitality displayed by Saunders was due to an adaptive adjustment to the brain changes revealed in the scans.

Discovery of brain atrophy on a routine scan could create a medical predicament, particularly if it is found in an apparently healthy individual who is performing his or her duties adequately or even successfully at a high level of responsibility.

Society as a whole, not just the medical profession, must accept the ubiquity and inevitability of brain failure. It has been suggested in the United States that leaders should undergo brain scans. There is a case for such a routine investigation to be directed towards the Good and Great who, without full examination including a brain scan, can be voted or promoted into the most responsible seats of government.

Chapter 6

Swings of Mood

There are many types and variations of mood, speech and behaviour associated with individualists, eccentrics or odd-balls whose action and mood remain within acceptable and tolerable limits. They need to be distinguished from the more serious, at times certifiable, anti-social swings which can be a danger to the individual and his or her associates.

It is probable that many with these less lethal behavioural disorders are detected in the middle grades of a government, bureaucracy, profession or military organization. They bring themselves to the notice of superiors early and rarely reach the highest rank. Although such behaviour may be due more to a character defect than a mood swing, it is revealing to consider the case of Lieutenant Commander Marcus Aurelius Arnheiter USN who took command of USS *Vance* in December 1965[1]. He found the destroyer crawling with cockroaches, her bridge and ladders stained with spilled coffee, and her crew brawling with the petty officers. Whilst he instituted daily inspections and compulsory church services, he violated Navy Regulations by keeping brandy in the officer's mess to pour over his peaches and cream. But it was his laudable desire for battle that disturbed his junior officers and led one to keep a 'Marcus Mad Log'. Despite orders to stay out at sea off Nam Quan, and cut off Vietnam traffic, Arnheiter ordered his officers to file false position reports. On around twenty occasions he sailed USS *Vance* close in to bombard shore positions and, on one occasion, within three hundred and fifty yards of the beach to blast a Buddhist pagoda which he suspected of being a Communist strong point.

His superior officers were probably informed of his over-zealous behaviour by the chaplain's corps since a Catholic officer had objected to the ship's services as a Protestant imposition. Early in 1966 Arnheiter was relieved and the Chief of Naval Personnel found him guilty of 'a gross lack of judgement and inability to lead people'. Relieved of his command, and relegated to a minor shore appointment, Arnheiter appealed but in November 1967 the Secretary of the Navy concluded that there was no valid reason to alter the decision.

The career of another middle-grade American officer illustrates the influence that innate personal and unconventional characteristics may have on public policy and safety. Colonel Oliver Laurence North, US Marine Corps attached to the National Security Council, drew himself to the attention of the world when, in 1988, he was a

61

key witness during the Tower Commission investigation into the
alleged arms deals between the United States and Iran.

In 1974 North, then aged 31, voluntarily entered Bethesda Naval
Hospital for treatment of emotional problems. He had just returned
from Vietnam and Okinawa and had been decorated with the Silver
Star and gained two Purple Hearts. His commanding officer had
found him at home 'babbling incoherently and running around
naked, waving a ·45 pistol'[2]. After serving in Vietnam he had gone
to the Naval War College where a chance meeting resulted in a
posting to the defence policy staff of the National Security Council.
His activities involved operations in Central America and Iran,
financial deals about hostages, diversion of funds to the Nicaraguan
Contras and the dramatic shredding of documents before his
appearance in front of the Tower Commission.

North was a compulsive worker, a go-getter, a workaholic of a type
appreciated by superiors until they are faced by the consequences
of such over-driven individuals. Such activity is not in any way
abnormal and does not feature in medical textbooks. North's
associates expressed themselves in non-clinical and crude terms,
saying that North was 'prone to hyperbole', something of a charlatan
and, by the summer of 1986, was so exhausted from eighteen-hour
days which allowed only three hours sleep that 'he looked like hell'.
Fact was mixed by North with fiction, he dropped names, especially
those of superiors. His fantasies included claims that he had been
a pre-medical student, fought in a special unit in Vietnam which
in truth had never existed, regularly met the President, had flown
a plane over El Salvador, served in Angola, gone with General
Alexander Haig to Argentina during the Falklands War and with
another American official, Philip Habib, to Israel in 1982.

Like so many of his type he impressed his superiors rather than
colleagues who thought him 'thirty to fifty per cent bullshit'[3] while
acknowledging the skill with which he 'cut through the bureaucracy
with his own special swagger'[4]. He was 'a whirling dervish'
whose 'swashbuckling Hollywood touches'[4], in particular, attracted
Reagan's attention. As for North's evasive answers about his alleged
unauthorized activities with the Director of Central Intelligence,
Joseph Persico, Casey's biographer, writes that 'Ollie stories took
on something of a Baron Munchausen quality within the national
security community'[5]. Another colleague spoke of his 'tendency to
engage in rhetorical hyperbole'[6].

It was inevitable that another member of this community would
refer to North's daytime, night-time and week-end activities as manic
days. It is essential to distinguish the boundless energy of a
compulsive worker like North from the mania or abnormal excitement
of the bipolar disorder which can swing from counterproductive
exaltation to depression. Fortunately it is rare, with annual hospital
admission rates in Britain of only around one per thousand of

the population. Minor types of mania, according to psychiatrists, may not be detected.

Unpopular or even popular personalities at all levels in government, politics, commerce or the powerful and secretive bureaucracies are often incorrectly called maniacal so that an awareness of precise psychiatric distinctions is essential. It is not a term that should be applied in exasperation or in fun to the exhausting but personally inexhaustible executives who may show at first sight, and on superficial assessment, at least some of the characteristics of the more lethal condition.

Perhaps the final verdict should rest with Robert C. (Bud) McFarlane, the National Security adviser, who worked, indeed conspired, closely with North over the diversion of funds to the Nicaraguan Contras. He himself took an overdose of valium during the Tower Commission investigation on 9 February 1987 and can speak with insight. In his opinion North 'was given to mood swings and idiosyncratic behaviour and occasionally deep depression'[25]. North, or his collaborator, deal with his behaviour in Bethesda Naval Hospital in a disarming way. North neither accepts nor denies the rumours; 'There were also stories about my hospitalization in Bethesda, including one report that I had been found running around naked—waving a gun![26].' His exclamation mark is a subtle touch.

Although General Norman Schwarzkopf disclaims heroism in his autobiography, there was a dark side to the genial and smiling image displayed to the world[28]. His terrifying tantrums and obscene public abuse of his officers in the Gulf War from 1990 to 1991 lowered morale. Even senior army commanders dreaded visits to his headquarters for fear of being 'clawed by the bear' when Schwarzkopf went 'ballistic'. It could have been sham rage but possibly a sign of his insecurity. Had Iraqi command, control, movement and supply not been crippled by air attacks, Schwarzkopf's behaviour could have been disastrous in a prolonged land battle[29].

For the perceptive, distinction between dangerous bipolar disorder should not be too difficult or impossible, although victims may present with any or all of a confusing variety of moods, thoughts and actions. They can be elated or irritable; full of ideas yet easily distractible with rambling speech; conduct is frenzied with a reduced need for sleep while their sexual activity and drinking may be unbridled; more important to others, inhibition and judgement are gravely impaired and they can spend and waste their own and other people's money in grandiose and impracticable schemes, many running concurrently and disastrously.

General (later Lord) Ismay showed in 1941 how a layman who has studied an individual can give a clinical description worthy of any medical consultant. As military chief of staff to Winston Churchill during the Second World War he described the prime minister:

'He is a mass of contradictions. He is either on the crest
of the wave or in the trough, either highly laudatory or
bitterly condemnatory; either in an angelic temper, or a
hell of a rage. When he isn't fast asleep he is a volcano.
There are no half measures in his make-up. He is a child
of nature with moods as variable as an April day[7].

Churchill described his down swings as his 'black dog' moods and
critics said that war was his therapy. In June 1941 the present Lord
Longford quoted Churchill's alleged daily prayer, 'O God, I thank
Thee for making me PM and grant that the war may last as long
as I live'[8].

But Churchill's moods, however extreme, were always within
acceptable limits although this must have been little comfort for
those out of favour. On 13 July 1943 Anthony Eden's private
secretary noted in his diary;

'The PM (Churchill) was in a crazy state of exultation. The
battle has gone to the old man's head. The quantities of
liquor he consumed—champagne, brandies, whiskies—were
incredible'[9].

Nor could Churchill's behaviour be excused on the grounds that
the battle was taking place on land, sea or in the air. It was only
a bureaucratic battle with the United States over recognition of the
new French Committee.

Churchill's reaction, however extreme and inappropriate in what
was merely a policy battle, could at worst be described as rationally
irrational and certainly not as the dangerous and abnormal
excitement of a manic–depressive psychosis. To those being driven
by a Churchill-clone, into actions and decisions about which they
professionally disagree, a differentiation between uncertifiable mood
swings and bipolar disorder may be academic. Fortunately the two
conditions are dissimilar both as regards current conduct and
outcome. They may be differentiated and compared, to use Churchill
again as an example, by citing his widely known consumption of
alcohol which was quite distinct from that of the confirmed and
unconstructive or destructive alcoholic.

Mania is a word far too easily and inaccurately applied to
adventurous individuals, often in commerce, when their empires fall
and ruin others. When Cyril Lord's carpet empire collapsed in the
1960s it was stated that he had a mania for cleanliness. He had much
of Churchill's boundless energy, urgency and enterprise and,
photographed wearing an astrakhan hat and smoking a cigar on
a visit to Moscow, he appeared a Churchill look-alike. Lord's
boundless energy, sense of urgency, nocturnal visits to his factories
because of sleeplessness and relaxation with tennis at six o'clock in

the morning were the physical, and not mental, causes of his collapse from high blood pressure as his empire passed to others.

In December 1930 the matron of a fashionable London nursing home made a retrospective diagnosis of Clarence Hatry, whose financial empire crashed in 1929. He had forged bearer securities, withheld payments from municipal authorities and duplicated the shares of some of his companies by bogus transfers. Despair and dishonesty were the more likely causes of his downfall and not what the matron called megalomania on the grounds that Hatry talked 'not in thousands or hundreds of thousands but in millions'[10] representing astronomical sums in the 1990s. It must be conceded that expansionist and creative endeavours may be undertaken by those whose attitude ranges from the ebullient to the euphoric. Hatry's enterprise was not curbed by his jail sentence of fourteen years. In prison he advised his wife on productive investments and, after his release in 1939, and over the next ten years he bought thirty bookshops, lending libraries, four printing companies and a publisher. True to form, he over-reached himself again and resigned from his companies because of what was called a nervous breakdown, but a bankruptcy petition was dismissed in 1953. He died in 1965 at the age of 77 after several attacks of coronary heart disease.

The tragic history of Peter Baker has much in common with that of Clarence Hatry but the differences do much to distinguish restless and imprudent overactivity with the even more serious implications and consequences of bipolar disease. After service with the embryo SAS in the 1939-1945 war, when he was captured by the Germans and interrogated by the Gestapo, his complicated commercial enterprises failed in 1954 when he was also a Conservative member of parliament. A patient in a mental hospital when arrested for forgery, he was sentenced to seven years' imprisonment. Four years after his release, in 1959, he became chairman of a literary agency which also failed financially. He died in November 1966 at the early age of 45.

His autobiography[11] is a grim and relevant reminder to colleagues and superiors that, whatever the difficulties, it is a dereliction of duty and responsibility to allow hyperactive, apparently tireless individuals to drive themselves, and at times others, to destruction. Entrepreneurs are human and not supermen. At one time Baker was the single manager of four publishing businesses, a printing works, a West End wine merchants, an aircraft research development and production unit, a proprietary brand of whisky, two investment trusts, a radio and television company and a property company.

Baker wrote of his 'obstinate courage that was near to madness'. In 1952 he was under the care of a cardiologist, gastroenterologist, neurologist and three other doctors. It was unpleasant and extremely expensive as 'they drugged me, injected me, massaged me and cajoled me' but could not persuade him to rest. Weeks passed in 1953 and

1954, before his eventual breakdown, which he could not remember. Later he was admitted to a nursing home after around thirty black-outs and two admissions to hospital for what he described as half-hearted suicide attempts. Baker's insight was profound and he wrote that 'my mind varied from unreliable pin-sharp brilliance to complete inability to record events and conversations'; and that 'eventually in the strange hinterland of overactivity and unremembered, unconnected exertions, a merciful cloud of unconsciousness descended upon me. The frenzy and the fury were over'.

In the nursing home he had cycles of collapse, recovery and semi-coma and on later admission to Holloway Sanatorium he was sedated for weeks. He regretted that 'my follies, my ill-judgements and, finally, my illness had cost a number of my friends and colleagues very dear'. How equipped were his friends and colleagues to assess his condition and take earlier steps to restrain him from personal and public indiscretion and disgrace?

The extreme and more dangerous forms of bipolar disorder are fortunately uncommon. Now that world leaders cannot avoid intrusive television cameras, bizarre behaviour on-camera is difficult to conceal. Yet that leading political diagnostician, Dr Pierre Rentchnick, a Swiss physician and medical editor, looked beneath the surface of Saddam Hussein's image. In November 1990 he watched a series of television interviews and was struck by the slowness of Saddam's response which he attributed either to tranquillizers or to some drug depressing the activity of the thyroid gland. His suspicions were confirmed by two British physicians who were passing through Geneva. They claimed that Saddam had been under treatment for some time for bipolar disorder during which he had swung into two depressive episodes; the first during the war against Iran and the second in the autumn of 1990. He had been correctly treated with lithium which, as an adverse effect, may have depressed his thyroid activity causing the sluggishness which was so apparent on the TV screen[12].

Diagnosis of public figures is now theoretically possible in open societies but TV cameras rarely penetrate government bureaucracies. Compared with Britain the United States is an open society and, as a result, the serious consequences of bipolar disorder in a senior member of the Central Intelligence Agency (CIA) have been made available to the world. Nor was this the work of a muck-raking journalist for many details were reported in a surprisingly revealing biography of Richard Helms, Director of the Central Intelligence Agency from 1966 to 1973. Paradoxically it is entitled 'The Man who Kept the Secrets'[13]. It says much for American openness that failings in their government servants are made known to the public rather than, as happens in Britain, concealed for fifty to one hundred years, or worse still, weeded and destroyed.

The life and death of Frank Gardner Wisner reads like a popular spy novel. A member of a secret organization formed in the Second World War, the Office of Strategic Services (OSS), he served in Bucharest in 1944 and, after the war, first with the State Department and later with the newly-formed Central Intelligence Agency (CIA). He became director of clandestine espionage at a time when immigration laws were manipulated so that anti-Communist exiles, some of them suspected Nazi war criminals, were brought to the United States, and then infiltrated back into Eastern Europe to eliminate Soviet police and Communist party cadres. In three years Wisner's CIA empire grew from three hundred staff in seven overseas stations with a budget of $4.7 million to two thousand eight hundred staff in forty-seven stations and $82 million budget. In 1953 Helms, who was then working under Wisner, proposed a study into the covert use of biological and chemical materials to control human behaviour.

In the late 1950s Wisner suffered two setbacks. 'The Company' as it is called had encouraged the hope of resistance among Hungarian emigrés and established stocks of arms but, when Khruschev sent tanks to Budapest in November 1956, American intervention proved impossible. Then half way through 1958 Wisner was held responsible for the CIA failure to subvert the Sukarno government in Indonesia; a CIA bomber supporting the rebels was shot down and the crew captured. In 1959 Wisner became Head of Station in London but retired from the CIA in 1961.

Wisner's medical history was equally dramatic. He is described as a man with 'incredible energy [who] drove his associates relentlessly'[14]. He worked hard, read widely, appeared to know everybody, argued intensely and, apart from complete involvement in all matters for which he was responsible, led an exhausting social life. He would ask several people to do the same job and then keep checking on each one. As these warning signs were intermittent they were ignored or shrugged away. At one dinner when Wisner had to speak his 'monologue ran on too long, was too repetitious, too heavy, tendentious, insistent'[13]. He was too easily distracted by irrelevant trivia and would ignore piles of urgent papers on his desk if he noticed a newspaper column with an incorrect heading. On his unhappy European trip in October 1956, coinciding with the Hungarian uprising, he rushed between appointments during the day, talked all night and hardly slept. Local American staff observed 'his odd, insistent, and at moments outrightly erratic behaviour'[13].

Wisner was 'unglued' after the Hungarian uprising in 1956 when 'he first went nuts' and called his colleagues 'a bunch of commies'[15]. It was around this time also that his drinking became excessive and he developed hepatitis, attributed to raw clams eaten in Athens. At a meeting at CIA headquarters in Langley to review the Hungarian tragedy Wisner continually interrupted the speaker to tell a lengthy and obscene story involving a male and female rest-room and lavatory paper. He had to be admitted to hospital where he demanded to ring the *Washington Post* about an idea for a cartoon. When a nurse said he was ill and it was too late at night Wisner threatened that he would set his goons on her.

After his trip to the Far East in 1958 and the Indonesian fiasco Wisner attended a 4th of July party where it was noted that he was talkative, overexcited and euphoric about some silk material which he had bought in Thailand[16]. Back in Langley he wrote lengthy and quarrelsome letters to friends and, at meetings, swung from monologues on obscure, irrelevant and unimportant matters to moody silence. After 1956 there had been episodes of depression and manic excitement and, in August 1958, he had a screaming attack at Langley and had to be restrained by ambulance men and taken to hospital. Following six months' treatment which included electroconvulsive therapy he returned to the CIA in 1959, served for a short period in London and retired in 1961. He continued to maintain contact with the CIA but, during another fit of depression in 1965, he killed himself with a twenty-gauge shotgun.

Chapter five of Thomas Power's biography of Richard Helms, in which he reviews Wisner's career, could well be used as a medical case study. It gives a vivid picture of bipolar disease which doctors in training would find more stimulating and practical than the usual philosophical and theoretical discussions about psychiatric disorders. Members of the CIA are carefully selected and are trained to observe and analyse. Yet, despite his bizarre conduct commented on by colleagues, no action was taken until he had to be physically restrained in 1958. So far as is known Wisner showed no evidence of the socially unacceptable and intolerable manifestations of bipolar disorder. It was only when he became physically violent that the men in the white coats were called to Langley. There were no reports of sexual misconduct, violence or financial profligacy though in the early 1950s when Wisner's department budget was 80 million dollars he asked why it could not be rounded off to 100 million.

The anti-social, even criminal, behaviour of some patients with bipolar disorder would presumably not be tolerated in political or bureaucratic life. The arts and literary worlds are more understanding and, indeed, creativity may be associated with or inspired by upswings in mood. Of some three hundred British painters, sculptors, playwrights, poets and novelists approached by Professor Kay Jamison, a University of California psychiatrist, forty-seven replied to questions about their mental state. Half the poets had been treated for depression or mania and Professor Jamison claims that artists and writers are thirty-five times more likely to be treated for mood disorders than the general population. Whitehall, Washington, Quai d'Orsay and Kremlin watchers should ask themselves whether the show-biz antics and misbehaviour have not on occasion been displayed by those with national responsibilities at all levels.

Robert Lowell, an American, may have been the best English language poet of his generation but he was violent to his schoolmates, father and women associates. In his manic attacks he foamed at the mouth, talked like a machine gun, shouted about devils and homosexuals and thought he could stop cars with his outstretched hands. On a cultural visit to Argentina in 1962 he drank six double vodkas before lunch, insulted the in-coming president during the meal and later visited the statues in Buenos Aires and insisted on climbing them in the nude. The laity on occasions seem well able to detect those oddities of behaviour which are part of manic hyperactivity. A friend who visited Lowell in hospital observed that in two hours he ate two pounds of chocolates and smoked two packs of cigarettes.

Much may be excused in the theatrical world but the hyperactivity of the British actress, Vivien Leigh, was characterized by sexual and general overactivity during which she hardly slept. Her loss of restraint, judgement, insight and reason involved her creating a scene in the public gallery of the House of Lords in Westminster, kicking a French actor in the testicles on stage and wrecking another actor's dressing room.

Unbridled hyperactivity with other manifestations in the life of a virtual dictator led to the collapse of the Philippine autocracy. The behaviour of Imelda Marcos certainly contributed to the downfall of her husband, Ferdinand, who had been president for over 20 years before his removal from power and exile in 1986. The rise and fall of Ferdinand and Imelda Marcos have been recorded in detail by an experienced journalist from the Philippines, Carmen Navarro Pedrosa, in a book published despite efforts by the Marcos couple to prevent its sale[17]. Described by Pedrosa as First Lady and co-dictator she lists the lavish schemes of Imelda Marcos allegedly funded by foreign or international bank loans, the Philippine National Bank out of intelligence accounts, unaccountable diversions from the World Bank and businesses taken over by decree, and other diversions of government loans and contracts. As Ferdinand Marcos became increasingly handicapped by renal failure Imelda in the last years 'was president in everything but name', in Pedrosa's view. Both had to leave a country in the depths of severe recession, debt and economic disaster with a poverty-stricken population welcoming Corazon Aquino as president.

Much has been made of the financial irregularities of the Marcos regime. In July 1991, however, she was acquitted in a New York court of charges that she and her husband had looted the country. On her return to the Philippines the authorities filed charges of tax fraud to enable them to recover 350 million dollars of ill-gotten gains which the Marcos family had deposited in a Swiss bank[18]. In

September 1993 Imelda Marcos was found guilty of corruption and sentenced to 18 years in jail. Unproven illegalities apart, her conduct was financially imprudent, irrational, uncontrolled and possibly uncontrollable by her husband or advisers. Pedrosa lists some of the centres she established at considerable expense; a Cultural Centre and also Population, Nutrition, Heart, and National Arts and Convention Centres. She built a series of monuments, bought a lavish mansion for the Marcos Foundation and was appointed Minister of Human Settlements by her husband. During these projects, behaviour indicative of her over-excited mental condition became apparent; she hardly slept, would ask for progress reports about building projects in the middle of the night and carried out pre-dawn visits to the construction sites.

Her spending reached a peak in 1982. The Manila International Film Festival involved the construction of a vast building and her state visit to Washington cost $30 million. When her youngest daughter was married in the small town of twenty thousand inhabitants where Ferdinand was born, she developed it in what she considered a 17th century style. The results were five new Colonial style buildings, guest houses, a reception centre, a new airport and a five-star hotel.

If confirmation is needed for a likely diagnosis of bipolar disorder it is given by Raymond Bonner in his investigation of the Marcos years[19]. In referring to her first state visit to Washington in 1966 he states that Imelda Marcos had made an earlier visit for psychiatric investigation. She was diagnosed as manic–depressive and treated first with tranquillizers and later with lithium, currently a specific treatment for bipolar disorder. At the time it was first noted that she only slept for three to four hours and her mental state explained, if it did not excuse, her buying sprees. In October and November 1977 in New York she spent nearly $1.5 million on jewelry, over $2 million in 1978, over $300 000 in 1979 and nearly another $1.5 million in 1981; to which must be added antiques worth $600 000 in 1981.

After the Marcos banishment Malacanang Palace, their presidential residence, was open to the public. What was in and around it did much to explain the fall of their regime. The lavish carpeting, furnishing and tapestries, and a cellar filled with antiques and objets d'art, might just be explained as legitimate if extravagant public expenditure. What was less excusable were three thousand pairs of shoes, two thousand ball gowns, five hundred brassieres, some supposedly bullet-proof, together with unopened boxes of handbags and gallons of anti-wrinkle cream[17]. Another report adds to her hoard a gold crown, three tiaras, sixty pearl necklaces, sixty-five gold watches, thirty-five rings, thirty-five racks of furs, two hundred black girdles and one thousand unopened packets of tights[30]. The five dialysis machines and oxygen cylinders were evidence of Ferdinand's renal disease and worsening incapacity.

But the most marked evidence of their regime's failure was the stench from the nearby river which, despite air-conditioning, could be smelt in the Palace. The river contains Manila's polluted waste and garbage from factories and slums along its banks. The atmospheric pollution should have reminded the ailing Ferdinand and the manic Imelda that the dissatisfaction of their poverty-stricken citizens would, sooner or later, end their dictatorship.

If bipolar disorder is uncommon, not only in secretive government departments but also in the outside world, another disorder may be more common in both the covert and overt activities. Mania is a word that may too often be used loosely but so too is paranoid, a term, if properly used, which means that an individual has a mental disorder marked by systematized delusions of persecution. Professor Desmond Curran, a distinguished British psychiatrist and once a consultant to a British official counter-intelligence agency, claimed that all staff referred to him for investigation were invariably paranoid. If officials are engaged and paid to question and suspect others, as well as their motives, they may justify their conduct, however extreme, on the grounds that they are discharging their obligations. When one looks at the secret world a balance must be struck and heed paid to Jim Hougan's warning that 'some writers are, in manner and method, spookier than those they investigate'[20].

It is hardly surprising that the CIA provides an outstanding, and in performance a counterproductive, example of a paranoid executive. At the same time the general public in Britain and other countries, where such incidents are buried by stringent laws of confidentiality, should not draw false comfort from the conclusion that such individuals are only to be found in American organizations. Any comparison between countries is impossible and the American revelations are due to the Freedom of Information Act which enables operatives to discuss such issues with responsible correspondents and authors. It is tempting, but fruitless, to speculate what is buried under the carpet not only in a reformed Russia but in Britain where, until John Major's *glasnost* in 1992, secret services did not officially exist though the location of their offices was widely known.

CIA operatives, together with psychiatric consultants from the organization, have been free to discuss the tragic case of James Jesus Angleton who for many years was in charge of its counter-intelligence activities. What may be called occupational paranoia led to the imprisonment and ill-treatment of Nosenko, who proved to be a genuine Russian defector, and even a growing suspicion about some members of the counter-intelligence staff and, in the end, of Angleton himself.

Dr Jerrold Post, now a professor of psychiatry and political psychology at George Washington University, and formerly a CIA psychologist who worked with Angleton, considered that he was not clinically paranoid but had 'a strong paranoid orientation and propensity'. Post considers that paranoia is 'a fixed conclusion searching for confirmatory evidence'. He adds that for paranoid individuals 'a clear, organized conspiratorial view of the world is easier for them to have since it gives them a sense of social security'[21]. By an unhappy coincidence Angleton's once favoured and alleged defector, Anatoliy Golitsyn, shared the same delusional system, as well as being allowed to share and study confidential reports on, from and about American and British agents, 'in a psychological folie à deux'. Angleton would tie together apparently unrelated world events and turn remote possibilities into certainty; to him there was no coincidence—'everything had meaning'. In support of Post, Dr John Gittinger, the CIA's head psychologist, diagnosed Golitsyn as clinically paranoid.

Professor Curran's clinical experiences with intelligence agents has been confirmed by Edmond Taylor, an American foreign correspondent and journalist, who drew on his experiences in the Second World War. He learned that officials in the secret world developed strange delusions about the aims and abilities of their opponents and, though he was not a psychiatrist, considered that their symptoms resembled clinical paranoia. Even soldiers, diplomats and statesmen were afflicted by what became permanent institutionalized delusions which became perpetuated as tradition or doctrine. They were difficult to recognize or remove because of 'a rigidity akin to that manifested by the delusive systems in the minds of real paranoiacs'[22].

Taylor is a layman but his opinion is supported by Dr Steven Pieczenik, a Washington psychiatrist, who was once a consultant to the State Department. Those in what he calls the political community require 'obligatory paranoia to operate effectively'; and 'they have to question other people's intentions, motives and manipulations to do their job'[4]. Difficulties unfortunately arise when they bring these acquired attitudes into their family or personal lives.

Whether paranoia comes down from, or floats up to, the top depends on individuals and circumstances. In December 1973, during Nixon's presidency, Admiral Elmo R Zumwalt, Jr, Chief of Naval Operations, told James Schlesinger, the Secretary of Defense, what he would say at the annual meeting between the president and the joint chiefs of staff. In the strongest terms Zumwalt was warned against any such approach for psychiatric reasons; 'To give a briefing like that in the White House these days would be just like shooting yourself in the foot. The president is paranoid. Kissinger is paranoid. Haig is paranoid. They're down on the Navy and to present facts like these to them will drive them up the wall'[23].

Paranoia on high is well illustrated by the case of Stalin's tea, which he drank all day. It was a whole-time job for a woman called Olga who held the key to a cupboard where the sealed packets were kept. She opened it under the eye of a supervisor who examined the pack to ensure that the stamp and seal were intact. The packet was then formally opened and surplus tea thrown away because it was forbidden to take tea twice from the same and now opened packet[24]. Stalin is an ideal candidate to be labelled as paranoid.

In 1927 the internationally respected Russian neurologist, psychiatrist and physiologist, Vladimir M Bekhterev, then aged 70, was called to the Kremlin by Stalin, who felt depressed. It is said that he diagnosed grave paranoia. As Bekhterev died that day or soon after, Stalin has come under suspicion. In 1989, however, Bekhterev's grand-daughter, a professor of neurophysiology, wrote that Bekhterev's second wife was suspected at the time, and it was only later that she could not dismiss the possibility that Stalin was responsible[27]. Paranoid or not, as he grew older, Stalin had excellent grounds for being morbidly suspicious.

Both the public and medical profession should be more aware of and sensitive to those with psychiatric problems. With understanding and foresight the manic-depressives might, by early intervention, be saved from themselves and the swings of mood which influence their conduct, their life and even death. As for those with paranoid traits, many people who are supposedly normal might be able to avoid their own manipulations which can condemn them to adjust to a paranoid distortion of reality.

Chapter 7

By Their Own Hands

The act of suicide, though now more discreetly reported in the press and regarded by the public with more understanding, is always a shocking event. What is more, such an outcome may be unexpected and not anticipated by relatives or close colleagues including those in the medical profession.

A suicidal league table has been provided by Dr Philip J Bohnert, an American psychiatrist from the Department of Family Medicine, Baylor College of Medicine, in Houston, Texas[1]. Those with primary affective disorder, namely severe depression, are twenty-five to five hundred times more likely to commit suicide compared with the general population. It should be realized that the downward swings of the less common bipolar or manic–depressive disorder represent a mere ten per cent of the total number of cases of depression.

Although suicide is widely, perhaps too easily, accepted as being associated with depression, there are other disorders which carry a risk of suicide higher than that in the general population. It is hardly surprising that AIDS, a relatively new entry, is next on Bohnert's league table (sixty-six times more common) followed by schizophrenia (thirty-four), substance abuse including alcohol (eleven to twenty), and diseases of the central nervous system including temporal lobe epilepsy (twenty-five) and multiple sclerosis (fourteen). New procedures beget new problems and the relative risks with renal disease and dialysis are ten to fifty times as high. Long-term disease brings its miseries but the suicide risk is as low as two to four times that of the general population in patients with cancer, three times more likely with respiratory disease but, surprisingly perhaps, two to nine times as high in those with peptic ulcers.

There are numerous signposts pointing to the risk of suicide but the potential victim may conceal them and casual observers may miss them because they lack the interest, insight or sympathy to penetrate the patient's protective screen. Paradoxically, the clinical picture may be so distressing or even repellent to unprofessional observers that they turn away with the excuse that they are untrained, or because the sight and sound threatens what may be their own brittle stability. The list of clues is long but their discovery needs a sympathetic approach and discreet questioning; hopelessness, loss of pleasure, panic, anxiety, depression, alcohol abuse, suicidal impulses, feelings of being a burden to others, ideas of persecution, fear of financial debts, a past history of admission to a psychiatric hospital and suicidal attempts. The divorced, widowed, unmarried and those living alone are also at greater risk than the rest of the population.

The difficulty of recognizing and accepting the likelihood of suicide, and the even greater problem of preventing or dissuading an individual from self-destruction, is illustrated by the death of Ernest Hemingway, the American writer. Admittedly there were many physical, rather than psychiatric, reasons for his general deterioration. In 1945 at the age of forty-six, Hemingway attributed his headaches, deterioration in patterns of thought and speech, and impaired memory to episodes of concussion. In 1956 his blood pressure and serum cholesterol were both seriously raised. When he returned to Spain in 1960 he displayed several features, prominent on Bohnert's list, with ominous indications. He had developed delusions of persecution and was frightened, lonely, guilty, full of remorse, and drinking heavily.

By November 1960 his blood pressure had risen again to 250/125 mm Hg but some of his depression was not unreasonably attributed to treatment with reserpine which was then the best available medication for hypertension. His increasing delusions, fears of destitution and harassment, depression and suicidal thoughts were more serious and predictive. Involved in a minor car accident, he feared that he would be imprisoned by the local sheriff. Driving past a bank he noticed that the lights were on and claimed that the staff were checking his accounts. What may appear to be ridiculous delusions must be considered with care. When in St Mary's Hospital, Rochester, Minnesota, for electroconvulsive therapy, he maintained that he was being watched by FBI agents; it was later found that this was not an irrational fear but was actually happening.

By April 1961 his intentions were all too obvious. He was found with a shotgun and two cartridges but Mary Welsh, his fourth wife, kept talking to him until his doctor arrived on a routine visit. On his way back to hospital later in the same month he tried first to shoot himself, then throw himself out of a plane and finally walk into the path of a taxiing aircraft on the runway. The sense of persecution persisted after discharge. On the way home he was certain that he was being tailed and, when wine was served at a picnic lunch, he stated that State troopers would arrest them for carrying alcohol.

Hemingway had thought of the act of suicide for at least twenty years. In 1940 he had justified it to Martha Gellhorn, his third wife, on the grounds that it was permissible in bad times. He actually enlarged on the method by which the bare toe could set off a shotgun trigger. It should therefore have been no surprise when on 2 July 1961 he placed the barrels of a shotgun against his own forehead and jerked both triggers.

Suicide is associated with the creative mood swings occurring in members of the arts, musical and literary worlds. It is certainly not expected in the military worlds whose members are carefully selected in the first place and trained and assessed over their careers before posting to increasingly demanding appointments. In the intense competition for the more limited opportunities for promotion in the years of peace, vulnerable individuals no doubt train themelves to conceal doubts, defects and insecurity. The least hint of weakness or, worse still, the seeking of medical or psychiatric advice would be difficult to conceal in close and highly competitive military communities.

Men and women are expendable in war but those who take their own lives deserve special consideration for they are the tragic few drawn from a potential pool larger and more vulnerable than is realized. Their case histories reveal how the all too common signs of unbearable stress, anxiety or depression are concealed by the victim and are ignored or not noticed by colleagues. The rigid discipline and necessary obedience of orders can lead to rough justice. In the heat of battle orders or actions can be miscontrued and there is no appeal for the man on the spot against defeat and censure. On active service there is a narrow line for all ranks between life or death, victory or defeat and honour or disgrace.

When studied retrospectively three case histories in particular should warn all officers to be aware that seniors, equals and juniors, unknown to colleagues, may be driving themselves or be driven to self-destruction. The dedicated, hyperconscientious and reserved back-room personality is particularly liable to stress, anxiety and insecurity which is kept concealed. In the summer of 1940, Captain E G Jeffrey became chief staff officer to Admiral Sir James Somerville then in command of H Force in the Mediterranean. The combination was foredoomed. Somerville was aggressive, quick-witted, impatient and talkative. He became irritated by Jeffrey's apparent lack of fire and slow thinking. In the autumn of 1941, when Somerville was away in Britain, Jeffrey hanged himself. He was a lonely introvert, unable to make friends, hypersensitive to criticism and anxious to please. He may have felt that his work was not appreciated and that the views of more confident juniors found more favour. It was a bitter irony that the high decoration, which he would have appreciated, was not announced until shortly after his death[2].

Not one but three reverses within a year shattered Captain Howard D Bode, United States Navy. In October 1941 he was head of foreign intelligence, US Navy department, reporting to Admiral Richmond K ('Terrible') Turner. Bode and a colleague urged that the intercepted Japanese 'bomb plot' message, which they recognized as an order to the Honolulu consulate to prepare for aerial attack by splitting Pearl Harbor into target areas, should be sent to the American service commanders there. Turner objected and was backed by Admiral H R ('Betty') Stark, Chief of Naval Operations[3]. It helped to seal Bode's fate as he was reassigned as Captain of USS *Oklahoma*. Although he was ashore on 7 December 1941 when she was sunk at Pearl Harbor, he became ironically one of the victims of his own ignored warning.

By August 1942 he was Captain of USS *Chicago* in a mixed force of American and Australian ships, commanded by a British Admiral, V A C Crutchley, which was supporting the landing of American marines on Guadalcanal in the Solomon Islands. Late in the evening of 8 August, Crutchley, commanding HMAS *Australia*, left the force with his flagship to confer with Admiral Richmond K Turner and Major-General Alexander Vandegrift, commanding the First Marine Division, and passed command of the southern of the three cruiser forces to Bode. Since Bode expected Crutchley to return before midnight he did not take station at the head of the force.

Meanwhile the Japanese eighth fleet commanded by Rear Admiral Gunichi Mikawa, after sailing down The Slot between the Solomon Islands and New Georgia, attacked the Southern Force south of Savo Island in the early hours of darkness on 9 August. Bode was wakened from a sound sleep and, after USS *Chicago* was struck by a torpedo, steered away from the main action because of gun flashes west of Savo. He failed to alert the Northern Force east of Savo and, later in confusion, USS *Chicago* fired on USS *Patterson*, which was standing alongside the stricken HMAS *Canberra*. This proved to be one of the worst defeats in United States naval history for, apart from the loss of HMAS *Canberra* of Southern Force, USS *Vincennes*, *Quincy*, and *Astoria* of Northern Force were sunk with heavy loss of life. Eastern Force was not engaged.

Bode retained his captaincy until the end of the year but in January 1943 was made commander of the naval station at Balbao, Canal Zone. After a preliminary investigation a full inquiry was begun in January 1943 by Admiral Arthur J Hepburn, a former Commander in Chief of the US Fleet, who because of illness spent the first three weeks in hospital. The inquiry found that Admiral Crutchley had over-emphasized the danger of submarines and air attack, disregarded that of surface action, and left the area without notifying his Northern and Eastern Forces. Admiral Turner had assumed that there would be an air attack in the morning. Both were guilty of bad judgement but were later exonerated.

After Bode was interviewed by Admiral Hepburn early in April 1943 he was quiet, tense, puzzled and surprised that his actions were being questioned. In a depressed state he returned to Panama, wrote a personal letter to Admiral Hepburn on 19 April and then shot himself. He died next day and his records are surely imprecise since they state that he was not a war casualty[4].

Suicide may be a threat even to the apparently successful commander. Rear-Admiral Don Pardee Moon, US Navy, the attack force commander on Utah Beach, Normandy, on 6 June 1944 became mentally and physically exhausted. Transferred to the Mediterranean theatre for Operation Dragoon, the amphibious landing in the south

of France in August 1944, he worried over the details of the plan
and what he considered the unreadiness of his force. After a series
of sleepless nights he begged Admiral H Kent Hewitt, Commander
of the Western Task Force, to postpone the new D-Day. After
Hewitt's reassurance, and his suggestion that they watch the
rehearsal and then consider any postponement, Moon appeared
satisfied on 4 August, but killed himself next morning[5].

Rear-Admiral Moon's susceptibility to the stress of operational
command was apparent to non-medical observers six months before
his suicide. They may not have realized that his introduction to war
in the West had been catastrophic and was a factor to be taken
seriously in any judgement of his capacity. In the summer of 1942
Moon, then aged fifty-two and a captain, was senior officer,
destroyers, in the Anglo-American convoy of thirty-six merchant
ships and nineteen warships called PQ17. On 17 June it sailed from
Iceland for Archangel in northern Russia carrying three hundred
aircraft, four hundred lorries, six hundred tanks and one hundred
and fifty thousand tons of general cargo. On 4 July PQ17 was ordered
to scatter, because of a threat from the German super-battleship
Tirpitz, by Admiral Sir Dudley Pound, the First Sea Lord at the
Admiralty, although he had previously been warned by Admiral Sir
John Tovey, commander-in-chief, Home Fleet, that such action would
be 'sheer bloody murder'[6]. Of the thirty-four merchant ships still
in convoy, only eleven reached Archangel. Pound took the decision
against the advice of all but one of his operational intelligence staff,
and it may have been influenced by the effects of a cerebral tumour
from which he died fifteen months later in October 1943. A witness
recalls 'a very tired looking Dudley Pound sitting gazing in a
mesmerized fashion' at a chart of the Barents Sea, closing his eyes
and giving the ill-fated order[7]. At the time Moon could not have
known about the originator of, or the reason for, the decision. Not only
must the destruction of PQ17 have been an unforgettable experience
but should have been a timely warning for the future, of the confusion
that can arise in an Anglo-American or any mixed command.

It was not until February 1944 that senior officers first became
aware of Moon's personality and its likely adverse effect on his
action, inaction, decision and indecision. In that month it had been
decided by the American high command to hold an invasion exercise
for the United States 7 Corps. The corps commander, General J
Lawton ('Lightning Joe') Collins immediately saw in Moon what
were 'disturbingly like weaknesses in a Naval Commander required
to make life or death decisions'[8].

Moon was anxiously over-diligent, a poor delegator, lacked
firmness and was too cautious. In Collins' words 'he is the only
Admiral I've ever met who wears rubbers on a mere rainy day'[9].
The practice for what turned out to be the landing on Utah
beach in Normandy on 6 June was called Tiger. It involved

twenty-five thousand men including US 4 Division and three hundred and thirty-seven ships making an assault landing on Slapton Sands, South Devon, which would involve the use of live ammunition and troops passing over mined beaches. Despite his innate caution Moon was unaware of the Anglo-American confusion likely to occur when an American force sailed through areas under British command. The assault was intended to be at 7.30 in the morning of 27 April, and the follow-up ships and stores would arrive in the area in the early morning of the 28th. Exercises are designed to find and remedy errors but the planning defects of Tiger compromised the operation before it began.

For example, the back-up convoy for Exercise Tiger was not given the United States or Royal Navy radio frequencies by Moon's staff and, through another failure of communications, a British escort destroyer with a vital role remained at Plymouth. In the early hours of 28 April German E-boats attacked the Tiger follow-up Convoy, sank two 'Landing Ship, Tanks' (LSTs) and killed over six hundred Americans. What was also disastrous, as later became apparent, Moon, with his tendency to indecision and delay, had moved the H-hour landing on the previous day (April 27) from 7.30 to 8.30 in the morning[10]. So strict a wartime and post-war censorship was later applied that some of the facts about the timings of the landing and where the casualties were sustained, and even where they were buried, have only been revealed by unofficial investigators in the 1980s. There is a strong suspicion that, through a lack of communication of Moon's H-Hour change on 27 April, some assault infantry landed at the original time of 7.30 and were killed by 'friendly fire' from the supporting artillery whose fire-plan had been postponed one hour to begin at 7.40 instead of 6.40.

Moon had actually wished to cancel the changed beach landing but his critic, Lawton Collins, of all people, prevented him from altering his plan and insisted that the landings went ahead. Moon was consumed by guilt, not so much about the E-boat assault on the night of 27/28 April, but for the troops killed on Slapton Sands on the morning of 27 April. His naval and army colleagues should surely have removed him, temporarily or permanently, from front-line service. It is hardly surprising that his familiar pattern of anxiety and procrastination continued during the actual D-Day landings in Normandy in June and, fatally and tragically for Moon, during the invasion in the South of France in August. His military colleagues can be excused from failing to anticipate his suicide. What is inexcusable was to allow him to continue as a Commander when his temperamental failings had already caused the death and wounding of those under his care and command.

Friends, colleagues and even political opponents working in closed communities, must often be aware of the signs that could give rise to suspicion about the mental or physical fitness of an individual.

Often appropriate action is avoided out of embarrassment or uncertainty about the best method of approach. Far too often the matter is avoided because it is conveniently dismissed as the responsibility of others.

The unhappy life and death of James Vincent Forrestal, the American Secretary of the Navy from 1940 to 1945 and the first Secretary of Defense from 1947 to 1949, have been analysed in a revealing book of nearly four hundred pages by Dr Arnold Rogow, an American political scientist. It was subtitled 'A Study of personality, politics and policy' for he emphasized factors external to the individual which may influence if not precipitate suicide[11].

In 1949 at the age of fifty-seven Forrestal's future was insecure and, although he had hoped to stay in office during President Truman's second term, he submitted, either voluntarily or by persuasion, his resignation on 1 March. After farewell ceremonies at the White House on 28 March his few close friends noted that he was agitated and depressed, declaring that he was a failure and contemplating suicide. He was convinced that certain communists, Jews and individuals in the White House were out to eliminate him and he developed the habit of searching his own house. Urged by colleagues to go away for a holiday in the company of his wife and friends he made at least one attempt at suicide. Nevertheless he improved sufficiently to joke that, as a precaution against suicide, his friends had to accompany him to the bathroom. Walking on the beach one afternoon, and pointing to the sockets used for attaching umbrellas, he warned against talking as their words would be recorded. His main fear was that the communists were about to invade the United States.

Medical consultations were arranged and a few days later on 2 April he was admitted to Bethesda Naval Hospital. On his journey from the airport to Bethesda, he behaved like Ernest Hemingway and had to be restrained from throwing himself out of the car. When he said on arrival that he did not expect to leave the hospital alive he could of course have been referring to suicide but also, in view of his fears, to murder. In contemporary terminology he was diagnosed as having involutional melancholia, or middle-age depression, a condition associated in a proportion of such patients with paranoid delusions. Forrestal was treated with heavy sedation, insulin therapy and daily psychotherapy.

His improvement allowed a relaxation of the close supervision which had involved the posting of a hospital resident doctor or orderly outside his suite on the 16th floor. He had told his psychiatrist on a number of occasions that if he did take his own life he would hang himself and not jump from a window.

On the evening of 21 May he told the naval orderly on duty that he did not need a sedative and would stay up late and read. In the early hours of 22 May Forrestal left his room, walked to the nearby diet kitchen, tied one end of his dressing gown sash to the radiator under the window and the other round his neck, and then jumped or hung from the window. Marks on the window sill and the wall underneath found later were a haunting reminder that he may have struggled to climb back. His body was found with the sash around his neck on the roof of a third floor connecting passage. There is even a possibility that his 16th floor suite was bugged, if only because Andrei Gromyko claimed that, before Forrestal jumped, 'he gave a frenzied cry; Russian tanks'[12].

The medical details gained or deduced from the histories of famous men and women invariably excite curiosity. Charity must be extended to their medical advisers who are dependent on the resources, investigations and treatment available and acceptable at the time. As in most types of historical inquiry retrospective conclusions and criticism can be grossly unfair to those concerned who are usually not able, even not alive, to refute any new theories and opinions.

Dr William Sargant, a leading British psychiatrist, agreed nearly twenty years after Forrestal's death with the diagnosis made in Bethesda Naval Hospital of severe depression with paranoid ideas. There were, and are, national differences in the treatment of illness and he questioned that given to Forrestal, particularly the psychoanalytical sessions. Apparently the US Navy psychiatrist who was responsible for Forrestal's care wished to treat him with electroshock therapy but a most distinguished psychoanalyst, with an international reputation, William Menninger, was against this approach. In the words of Dr William Sargant, Forrestal 'was talked to until he threw himself out of the window'[13]. He is quoted as saying in a lecture that Forrestal was inadequately treated as the medical staff were in awe of him because of his high status. It was also rumoured that recommendations that Forrestal be confined to a locked room were ignored because the patient objected and, more important, President Truman issued an unverified executive order that no cabinet minister should be confined in that manner. Unfortunately the naval doctor, Captain George Raines, who was primarily responsible for Forrestal, saw his patient for the last time on 18 May, and was away at a professional conference when the suicide occurred.

What is particularly disturbing to learn from the points of view of early diagnosis, treatment and prevention is that Forrestal's deterioration, although it worsened rapidly after his last good-bye in the White House in March 1949, had begun at least one year before. Some of his friends were disturbed about his loss of appetite and weight, so-called stomach trouble, insomnia and exhaustion. In March 1948 they also noticed odd behavioural mannerisms which naturally they could not assess. Strange habits developed such as dipping his finger into liquids and moistening his lips and also continued scratching of his scalp. After apparent acceptance of decisons or documents he would reconsider and change them.

When President Truman learned at the end of 1948 that Forrestal thought his phone was being tapped he ordered the Head of the Secret Service, U E Baughman, to investigate. Baughman questioned Forrestal's domestic staff and learned from the butler that his employer had become suspicious of visitors and was generally confused. Baughman also discovered that Forrestal had bought sleeping tablets and, though not medically qualified, concluded in his report to Truman that Forrestal had sustained a psychotic breakdown with suicidal tendencies. From the point of view of the medical profession it is distressing to learn that Forrestal had a routine check-up at the Walter Reed Hospital on 8 February 1949 at 3 o'clock in the afternoon, and attended again two days later. For personal reasons he may have been reticent and understandably reluctant to discuss his apprehension, frustration and feelings of injustice. Again with the benefit of hindsight his appearance and manner surely provided significant clues, if not to the final diagnosis, at least to further investigations.

What probably negated the routine medical examination, or even further more detailed check-up, was that any efforts by his doctor, colleagues and friends, together with the political establishment, were nullified by the universal and ever-present doctrine which denies that a VIP can become physically, let alone mentally ill. Rogow lays the blame on the mental health mythology of Washington and 'the denial that any Very Important Person can become mentally ill while in office'. As a result it is accepted that ordinary people become psychotic, 'VIPs do not', ordinary people 'who can afford it' visit psychiatrists 'but not VIPs' and ordinary people may spend time in mental hospitals 'but never VIPs'[11].

Forrestal's suicide occurred over forty years ago but Rogow's research must not be treated as past history and its lessons forgotten. It is a tiresome platitude to point out that history repeats itself. Yet there is a link between certain psychological adjustments made by Forrestal in the 1940s and those of Angleton in the 1960s. Rogow's study of Forrestal appeared in 1963 when Angleton and his staff in counter-intelligence were dazzling others and being dazzled themselves in what has aptly been called a wilderness of mirrors. Rogow points out that 'Forrestal's personality needs and policy recommendations were closely related', his fears and uncertainties eased by a harsh anti-Soviet attitude which fitted the current political climate. Despite his abnormal behaviour he could still be rated as reasonable because in the atmosphere of the Cold War it was understandable to be suspicious, to advise caution about any adjustment or agreement about differences and to speak of the need for confrontation.

Suicide at the top is uncommon and when it does occur most commonly involves members of a defeated dictatorship or putsch. Hitler, Goering, Goebbels and Himmler, together with generals and culpable officials, thus saved themselves from a lengthy trial and certain execution. The prospect of such a fate presumably led President Getulio Vargas of Brazil to take his own life in August 1954 at the age of seventy-one. He had been provisional or elected president from 1930 to 1945 and a virtual dictator of the totalitarian new state from 1937. Overthrown in 1945 he returned to power in January 1951 but in 1954 the armed forces, shaken by the scandals associated with his regime, joined in a call for his resignation.

Autocratic individuals in other fields may turn to suicide when they are faced, not only with loss of power and influence, but with the collapse of their financial empires and loss of the monetary addiction which was their main stimulus. Suicide in this group seemed to be more fashionable between the two world wars. When Captain Alfred Loewenstein, a Belgian, realized that his companies were about to fail he walked out of his aeroplane over the middle of the English Channel on 5 July 1928. Ivar Kreuger, the Swedish financier, not only controlled sixty-five per cent of the world match production but set up over four hundred subsidiary companies, often only a name on an office door, but others with faked ledgers to falsify each others' books. After the Wall Street crash of 1929, and the financial collapses in Europe, he turned to forging Italian treasury bills and certificates of indebtedness. It may have been a detective from J P Morgan, the American financier, whose threat of exposure led to Kreuger shooting himself in 1932, though some claim either that Kreuger was murdered or alternatively that he disappeared to Sumatra and an available corpse buried in his name.

There are similar doubts about the cause of death of Alexandre Serge Stavisky, a Russian, who came to France before 1914, and served prison sentences for fraud despite later protection by influential contacts among the police, judiciary and politicians. When an immense issue of fraudulent shares brought protests from defrauded investors in 1934, Stavisky was traced by police to Chamonix. As they forced the front door they heard a shot and found Stavisky with a wound in his head from which he died next day. As with Kreuger his act of suicide is questioned and it is believed that he was shot on orders of certain politicians.

The sudden death of Robert Maxwell in November 1991 led to immediate debate about the probability of accident, suicide or even murder rather an acceptance that it could have been due to 'natural causes'. The exposure of the massive failure and financial misappropriation in his crumbling empire will ensure that theories or revelations about his death will provide material for books and newspapers in the years ahead.

Compared with the suicide of political or military leaders overwhelmed by the rush of events, or those of potential war criminals, plotters against the state or failed financiers, that of Egerton Herbert Norman, the Canadian ambassador, in Cairo at the early age of 48 marked the end of a tragic sequence of events[14]. Until the fatal 4 April 1957 his career appeared to be a model for any diplomat. After graduation from the University of Toronto, he took a second degree at Trinity College, Cambridge, in 1935 and then won a Rockefeller Foundation fellowship in Far Eastern studies at Harvard University. Due no doubt to his Japanese academic studies he was posted to Tokyo as a language officer in the Canadian Embassy and, on his repatriation after Japan's entry into the war in December 1941, served in the department of External Affairs in Canada where he formed a Japanese intelligence section.

From 1946 to 1950 he was head of the Canadian Liaison Mission with General Douglas MacArthur headquarters in Japan. Back in Canada again he became head of the American and Far Eastern division at External Affairs, took part in the conference on the Japan peace treaty but in 1952 he was moved to the less sensitive Information Division. In 1953 he emerged into the limelight again as High Commissioner to New Zealand and, on the advice of Lester Pearson, then secretary of state for external affairs and a later prime minister, rejected a university appointment, and remained in external affairs until he became ambassador to Egypt.

From 20 April 1950, when his name was mentioned in a US Senate Committee investigating alleged disloyalty in the far eastern staff of the State Department, and his death in April 1957, Herbert Norman lived a life periodically shattered by allegations and innuendoes about disloyalty and communist associations. In August 1950 counter-intelligence departments in Washington and Tokyo compared notes about Norman who, during his posting in Tokyo, had attracted attention by his association with, and release of, left-wing individuals, and his contribution to what were regarded as subversive publications. In September, J Edgar Hoover of the FBI first approached the authorities in Ottawa. In 1942 Norman had unwisely put himself in the FBI records by using his official status to acquire the books and papers of a supposedly communist Japanese classmate who had left them behind in Cambridge, Massachusetts. Norman finally had to admit to the FBI agent that his quest was for personal and not official reasons.

In October 1950 an erroneous Royal Canadian Mounted Police (RCMP) report on Norman, which the RCMP later disavowed, was given by the FBI to the Senate Subcommittee on Internal Security (SSIS) and became the basis of the Senate's public accusations against Norman in August 1951. Another RCMP report in December 1950 stated that the worst possible conclusion was the naiveté of his human relationships. A further report for the department of

External Affairs in January 1952 concluded that he had been a communist in opinion, an active party member, had associated with communists and, hardly surprising in view of the cell in Trinity College, Cambridge in the 1930s, his belief dated from 1935. He was cleared but doubts lingered despite his loyalty to the government being affirmed privately in December 1950 and February 1952 and publicly in August 1951 and March 1957.

It was ironical that John K Emmerson, an old American friend from his days in post-war Japan, mentioned his name and present appointment on 14 March 1957 during congressional hearings in Washington by the Senate Subcommittee on Internal Security. Although Lester Pearson in the Canadian parliament denied the renewed charges from Washington, Norman became preoccupied, tense, lost interest and appeared disturbed. The Cairo embassy staff thought he must be sick as his behaviour had 'changed alarmingly', he barely participated in discussions and did not appear to be 'mentally with us'[14]. An embassy servant was asked to open the door to the Chancery roof and watched Norman looking over the side.

Early in the morning of 2 April he called on Dr Halim Doss, his personal doctor in Cairo who was not immediately available, and in a distressed condition asked Mrs Doss if he could see whether the verandas of the penthouse apartment were, in fact, enclosed in glass or wire mesh. His statement that he had come to commit suicide may have been, as his biographer writes, 'his last cry for help'. Later Norman told Dr Doss about the SSIS allegations, the RCMP investigations in 1950, his ties with communism and the suicide notes he had written. Nearly thirty years later Doss remembers Norman saying that he 'was as near to having been a communist without being a communist as one can be'. More relevant, however, was his statement that he could not face a third RCMP interrogation. Rest and sedatives were advised but on 4 April he took the lift to the eighth floor of the Wadi el Nil building overlooking the River Nile and threw himself from the roof. As Norman said to an American friend 'innocence is not enough'.

His suicide was almost inevitable and certainly not preventable as he had been under intolerable strain for seven years. Whether this was a result of his past communist associations, even misconduct, can now only be a matter of opinion. Cleared by the Canadian government he came under sporadic, damning and unexpected attacks from counsel or witnesses in US Senate committees. In a private letter after the suicide Lester Pearson wrote that Norman's mind gave way under pressure of work and the revival of charges five years after he had atoned for his communist illusions and mistakes. During his consultation with Dr Doss on 2 April Norman admitted that Lester Pearson's clearance of him in 1952 after the first SSIS allegation was misleading. Indeed Norman's widow, Irene, said that his suicide was unselfish, heroic and stupid but was done to protect Pearson for withholding evidence in 1951. Howard Norman maintained that his brother's suicide was due to sickness from overwork, the tragic issues of the Suez crisis when his excellent relations with Nasser enabled him to play an important role, and a morbid anxiety, both for Pearson and himself, that the concealment in 1951 about his recruitment to communism at Cambridge would be exposed.

The secret world is a wilderness of mirrors. Those eminent spy-watchers, John Costello and Chapman Pincher, claim that Norman was a KGB agent. Their view is supported by Peter Worthington, a Canadian journalist, who is also suspicious of Pearson both for his suppression of information about Norman and because a communist courier claimed to have been the link between Pearson and Norman. But the mirrors give other images. In one of his suicide notes Norman wrote, 'There are forces bent on my destruction—*and I am not suffering from a persecution complex*' (his italics). In a letter to the British *Daily Telegraph* on 9 April 1990 Professor Peyton Lyon of Ottawa wrote that the Central Intelligence Agency had faked two of Norman's suicide notes whilst an astutely inventive paragraph in a CIA message from Cairo made it appear that Norman was thinking of escaping from new and incriminating disclosures. Needless to say this was denied later by Robert Crowley, a former CIA operative[15].

The words of the American writer, Daniel Webster, can surely apply to all who take their own lives; 'There is no refuge from confession but suicide; and suicide is confession'. It could be argued that Norman's confession in 1951, influenced possibly by Lester Pearson, was never fully revealed, and the half truth could not be remedied by his last act.

Sometimes lessons are learned from past tragedies. In 1967 Robert McNamara, the coldly calculating number-cruncher, resigned after six years as US Secretary of Defence. Senator Goldwater later wrote that McNamara 'intellectualized and computerized all issues' even human ones, reduced problems to cost-effectiveness and logistical numbers, was always massaging and manipulating data, 'selected managers, not leaders', and never visited troops in the field[16].

Although McNamara insisted that 'you can never substitute emotion for reason' the facade of 'rational self-confident efficiency' could no longer conceal that he was wilting under the strain of the escalating war in Vietnam. The fate of a predecessor who served as Secretary of Defence, James Forrestal, may have warned his friends that McNamara might actually take his life after he had resigned[17].

President Lyndon Johnson was worried about 'another Forrestal'. One observer noticed that 'his speech was vague and he rambled aimlessly as he talked'. For others 'the comparison with Forrestal was becoming too real'[18].

It is only to be hoped that the public as well as the medical profession learn from what might be potentially preventable tragedies. Those who are deferentially regarded as iron men and women, subjected to what may have become unbearable stress, may conceal even from close associates their potentially lethal feelings of hopelessness, despair and futility.

Chapter 8

Hearts and Minds

By the 1930s the expanding art and science of cardiology was making diagnosis more precise. It was particularly helpful in coronary thrombosis, now usually called myocardial infarction, which was increasing in incidence. The developing technique of electrocardiography was another aid to rapid diagnosis but analysis of its recordings was not free from error. In the 1960s Henry Marriott, a British cardiologist practising in Florida, warned that certain wave patterns on an electrocardiogram could lead physicians astray as they were examples of what he called coronary mimicry[1]. They were only normal variants arising from physiological, pharmacological or pathological factors which could simulate the electrocardiogram (ECG) changes generally accepted as recording coronary obstruction. A mistaken interpretation could force a healthy individual into sheltered employment, early retirement or a half-life of cardiac invalidism.

There were (and always will be) exceptional patients who defied medical advice or restrictions and lived normal lives, however brief. Later surgical advances such as heart-valve replacement, coronary artery by-pass procedures, or clearance of coronary obstruction by other methods, could return a patient's cardiovascular function virtually to normal.

In the 1960s it was first appreciated that in coronary artery disease a patient's personality could be the cause not only of the cardiac problem but also of character traits which shaped the patient's behaviour, decision-making and way of life. Friedman and Rosenman described a Type A personality characterizing the possessor as being intense with a sustained drive for achievement, continually involved in competition and achieving deadlines. Compared with their Type B opposites, the Type A personality was associated with a raised serum cholesterol, an arcus senilis at the margin of the cornea and a raised incidence of coronary thrombosis[2]. They later described Type A behaviour as an 'action–emotion complex' in which the individual engaged in a 'relatively chronic and excessive struggle to obtain a usually unlimited number of things from his environment in the shortest period of time or against the opposing efforts of other things or persons in the same environment'[3]. Their views on the psychosomatic aspects of ischaemic (coronary) heart disease became generally accepted[4]. Type A personalities may well predominate in those who strive for and gain power. Some may persist despite cardiac disability. Others, whose cardiac problems have at least been temporarily resolved by advances in cardiac diagnosis and vascular surgery, still retain both the political advantages, and, at times, disadvantages of a Type A personality.

The difficulties posed by such a patient with cardiac disease are starkly revealed by the medical history of General H H Arnold, appointed commanding general of the US Army Air Force in 1942 at the age of fifty-six years. In February 1943, after intercontinental flights under wartime conditions to India, China and North Africa he developed chest pain on his return to America after a 'rather heated argument in the White House'[5]. Despite his objections he was transferred to the Walter Reed Hospital outside Washington where a severe coronary thrombosis was diagnosed.

Arnold was only too well aware that if a serious illness was entered into his medical record it might lead to forced and early retirement. Army regulations would not normally permit active service with such a medical history but President Roosevelt as commander-in-chief could make the final decision. It was fortunate that Roosevelt was advised by Henry Stimson, Secretary of Defense, and General George C Marshall, the US Army Chief of Staff. The former was an unfit seventy-six-year-old whilst Marshall, who had had a thyroidectomy in 1936, told Lord Moran in August 1943 that he was having attacks of atrial fibrillation[6]. Roosevelt was advised that Arnold's routine and flying put his life at risk but, as this applied to his aircrews, Roosevelt allowed him to remain.

Within three months he had a second heart attack, a third in May 1944 and a fourth in January 1945. Nevertheless he set out on a visit to the European theatre of operations in March 1945 as it was considered that the trip would be more relaxing than the continual battles in the Pentagon. His European activities became so frenzied that General Marshall asked him; 'where is the Bermuda rest, the lazy days at Cannes, the period of retirement at Capri? You are riding for a fall, doctor or no doctor'[7].

It could also be claimed that Arnold's four attacks of coronary thrombosis were related to his personality. Although he also had hypertension, and was on medication because his pulse rate rose to 160 during his second coronary thrombosis, he was 'energetic, restless, quick, impatient, hard driving'[7], a perfect description of the Type A personality. It was his personality that caused an unfortunate staff colonel to drop dead while Arnold was abusing him about allegedly inaccurate figures.

It was also Arnold's personality that led to two disastrous bombing raids by the US Air Force. After his first heart attack Arnold returned to Washington on 21 March 1943 and three days later took a rapid decision about US Air Force operations in Europe. He advised its commander that the destruction of the German ball-bearing factories would have a greater influence on reducing industrial production than attacks on other targets. Of 230 B-17 Flying Fortresses which took part in the daylight raid on these factories around Schweinfurt on 17 August 1943, thirty-six were destroyed. There was worse news to come. Of the 291 Flying Fortresses sent on the second daylight raid to Schweinfurt on 14 October 1943, sixty (and six hundred crew) were shot down while a hundred and forty-two of the two hundred and thirty-one which returned to England were damaged.

Arnold's christian names were Henry Harley and, possibly in view of his lethal abuse, he was nick-named 'Hap' (not Happy). Life assurance actuaries would have been concerned with his cardiac history, hypertension and fibrillation, rather than his Type-A temperament which had a direct influence on these. Yet he lived until the age of sixty-four.

Whether the Type A personality is congenital or acquired its aggressive and, at times, self-destructive manifestations are difficult to control or explain to the victim. Even in military personnel and those senior business executives, subject to routine physical checks, its undesirable and counter-productive effects are also difficult to prevent. Nevertheless, little action is taken against those in executive and military authority whose physical and temperamental incapacity may have disastrous national and international effects.

In 1992 two exhaustive studies of the available medical records and medical histories of American presidents revealed that General (later President) Eisenhower could well have been a Type A personality[8,9]. It may have been responsible not only for his rise to supreme power in two different fields of endeavour but also for his cardiac and vascular problems. The two authors each conducted independent research, studied records uncovered relatively recently and drew similar conclusions. Much had clearly been concealed by the Eisenhower family, the White House, and his principle physician.

Robert H Ferrell[8], an emeritus professor at Indiana University and author of books on American presidents, reveals that Eisenhower came from a family with a history of hypertension and one imbued with a drive for high achievement. What was long presumed to be the first infarction on the night of 23/24 September 1955 occurred a few hours after a fit of rage when he was summoned three times to the telephone from a golf course by callers who had hung up, were not available or were non-existent. There had already been ominous symptoms and signs. As early as 1943 his blood pressure was found to be raised and in 1947 there was a sudden episode characterized by dizziness, difficulty in standing, and raised blood pressure. This was attributed to bleeding into the semicircular canals of the inner ear. On 21 March 1949 another illness was publicly diagnosed at the time as gastroenteritis. In 1983, Dr Thomas W Mattingly, an Army cardiologist, who was adviser to Eisenhower from 1953 until his death in 1969, found in a file of records a single electrocardiogram dated 5 April 1949. Precise diagnosis was not possible but the tracing suggested myocardial damage. Furthermore, on 16 April 1953, during his first term, Eisenhower was affected by what was dismissed as food poisoning but which Mattingly, years later, was sure must have been another heart attack.

Ferrell mentions Eisenhower's excessive smoking, ill-temper, his shouting at officers as senior as General Douglas MacArthur, and a generally stressful life. Mattingly concluded that Eisenhower had a Type A personality. Although nominally acting as Eisenhower's cardiologist his contacts were selective and he only saw him when the president's chief physician from 1945 to 1961, General Howard A Snyder, called him into consultation.

Gilbert[9], a professor of political science, in an equally exhaustive study provides confirmatory evidence of the contemporary concealment of Eisenhower's illnesses and the issue of highly selective bulletins. Gilbert concludes that Eisenhower had an obsessive and compulsive personality, drove himself to work fourteen-hour days and seven-day weeks, and only took leave when ordered by his seniors. A final and precise diagnosis can never be made because of the intractable problem of Henry Marriott's 'coronary mimicry'. Although Eisenhower's electrocardiogram in 1949 was suggestive of myocardial damage, painstaking research by Gilbert has revealed that as late as 1984 Mattingly revised his original opinion that Eisenhower's illness in 1949 was necessarily due to a myocardial problem. He admitted that exactly similar electrocardiographic changes to those seen in 1949 were also apparent in the 1947 and 1951 tracings; 'indicating that they were chronic configurations and not the result of resolving changes of a recent myocardial damage'.

Eisenhower's medical history certainly confirms that accusations of concealment from the public, especially before elections, can justifiably be levelled. In defence it can be claimed that for humane reasons the truth may be concealed solely out of concern for the patient's welfare. More relevant, perhaps, because of the limitations of diagnostic procedures the final diagnosis may unfortunately be obscured, and conscientious and ethical physicians be accused of unethical concealment.

There is an apocryphal story of a pregnant woman wandering around the floors and corridors of the Pentagon. Told that she should not be there in her condition the reply, that she was not pregnant on arrival at the Pentagon, is applicable in another context to senior officers of the armed forces. It raises the question whether four star officers have normal personalities on arrival but switch to Type As owing to the competitive and stressful way of life. The career and medical history of General Earle G ('Bus') Wheeler is indicative of a lack of care, concern for, and control of senior officers in key positions. Wheeler was appointed as chief of staff, US Army, in 1962 at the age of 54 and, in 1964, as chairman of the joint chiefs of staff. He held this supreme command until 1970 and therefore was closely involved in the increasing commitment of US forces at home and abroad as well as the size of the forces in Vietnam. Between 1967 and

1970 he was clearly unfit to take strategic decisions or indeed to hold any responsible position. In August 1967 he had a heart attack which was at first concealed[10]. It was the 'first of many that would eventually kill him'[11]. When he returned to duty in October 'he looked terrible', according to his aide, 'as if he would rather have been anywhere else'. A second lay opinion was given by Admiral Thomas H Moorer, chief of naval operations and a close colleague, who remembered him as 'a very sick man'[11].

On Wheeler's fourth visit to Vietnam in February 1968 General William Westmoreland, the local US commander, considered him 'an exhausted and ill man'. He was no longer erect, stalwart, alert and handsome but haggard, gray, tired and pot-bellied[12]. He was not physically or mentally capable of easing the exaggerated fears of President Johnson and the Pentagon, fanned by the United States media, about the Tet offensive launched on 1 January 1968. Westmoreland was certain that the offensive had been contained. This was not what Wheeler wanted to hear. He wished to create the impression with the President that Westmoreland had asked for reinforcements so that he would have a reason to call up the Army reserves to resolve his own fears about possible emergencies in Berlin, the Middle East or, worse still, anti-war demonstrations, race riots and other civil disturbances in the United States. Wheeler always denied that he had intentionally misled the President[12]. It is clear that he needed an excuse, which Westmoreland did not or could not provide, to justify a call-up of reserves[13]. As chairman of the US Joint Chiefs of Staff Wheeler had worldwide responsibility. In a speech which he made in Detroit in December 1967 he mentioned Westmoreland's warning of a possible North Vietnam offensive, but concentrated on the dangers of a US anti-war movement.

At the beginning of 1969 Wheeler's increasing incapacity put a strain on the Joint Chiefs of Staff and he had to share his duties with Admiral Moorer. By the late summer Wheeler was obviously 'slowed by heart disease'[11] but, despite another episode of illness in April 1970, he stayed in office until his retirement in July 1970 at the age of sixty-two. He died from a heart attack in 1975.

Wheeler's increasing incapacity may be a charitable explanation for a convenient lapse of memory in 1968. Summoned by the Senate Foreign Relations Committee, and asked whether in 1964 two US warships had been ordered to bait and provoke the North Vietnamese, Wheeler replied; 'to the best of my knowledge there was no thought of extending the war into the north'[15]. During Wheeler's last year in office Henry Kissinger provided a literary and almost spiritual view of his appearance, stating that Wheeler was deeply disillusioned but adding: 'he looked like a wary beagle, his soft dark eyes watchful for the origin of the next blow'[16]. Ironically, two weeks before he retired on 2 July 1970, he was involved in a decision about a secret operation which resulted in a fiasco in November 1970. A helicopter force, landing in and around Son Tay prison twenty-three miles from Hanoi, found that the sixty-one prisoners, whom they had flown to rescue, were not there[17].

It can always be argued that between 1967 and 1970 any other, supposedly fitter, chief of the Joint Chiefs of Staff would have come to the same conclusion and decision about a reserve force. It is Wheeler's tactics that are open to criticism and the only explanation or excuse available is that his physical and mental incapacity played an important part in 'one of the most devious and damaging episodes in American military history'[12].

If unfit generals, serving in a disciplined community, cannot be taken off duty by the checks that apply to the lower ranks, any medical control or restraint of leading politicians can hardly be expected. Admittedly advances in cardiac therapy and resuscitation have enabled younger leaders not only to survive but to continue in office. In 1974 the fifty-five-year-old Helmut Schmidt became Chancellor of the Federal Republic of Germany in succession to Willy Brandt who retired prematurely in May. This was variously attributed to the return of a severe depression, first reported after a heart attack in 1965, the revelation that an East German secret agent was a close adviser, but also to a mental condition rare in leaders, *Amtsmüdigkeit*, weariness of office. Brandt's various illnesses, only two years before, had been widely reported in the German press. There were alleged viral infections, fever, loss of up to 12 kg in weight, hand tremor and excessive sweating. At that time he was Minister of Defence and explained that, as he was working sixteen hours a day, 'nobody can stand this murderous job for a long time'[18]. Virus infections may have been a cover story to conceal the real problem. He had to treat his ocular protrusion with eye drops and early in 1972 a thyroid disorder was diagnosed which responded to daily and continuing treatment.

Schmidt was Federal Chancellor from 1974 to 1982 and in 1981 his general condition deteriorated. Far from *Amtsmüdigkeit* he manifested Schmidt Schnauze' outbursts of rage. His devoted followers called him Super Schmidt and, those he abused, Schmidt the Lip. He smoked eighty cigarettes a day and in 1977 that perceptive diarist, Roy Jenkins, saw Schmidt, joined by Princess Margaret, at a Buckingham Palace banquet smoking before the main course and stubbing out his cigarette ends on a 'very high quality plate'[19]. More significant, Jenkins recorded on 31 January 1980 that Schmidt was complaining about his health and 'apparently has some nasty form of angina'.

It should therefore have not surprised the world press that on 12 October 1981, two days after returning from President Sadat's funeral in Egypt, he was flown with the customary cover diagnosis of a virus infection to Koblenz Military Hospital. He had lost consciousness several times at home on 11 October and was unconscious when admitted to hospital, according to Dr Wolfgang Völpel his personal doctor. Reports from the newspaper *Bild* which claimed that Schmidt's heart had stopped four times in hospital, and that he had experienced black-outs since July, were understandably described as exaggerated or incorrect by Manfred Lahnstein, the head of the Chancellery. Schmidt returned to duty in a few days but his memory for recent events was poor although his past recall was unimpaired. Although he was due to serve another three years he gave up the chancellorship in 1982, becoming editor-in-chief of *Die Zeit* in 1985. His prudent response was an example to ailing leaders who, after treatment, may well be capable of less demanding posts, but certainly not for supreme command. Indeed, recent surgical advances, while improving a patient's cardiovascular function, may as an unexpected and unfortunate side-effect adversely impair personal behaviour.

In January 1981 General Alexander Meigs Haig, Jr, faced questioning by the foreign relations committee of the United States Senate with regard to his appointment as Secretary of State. One experienced journalist, James Reston, wrote that some observers were doubtful because although Haig in civilian clothes looked like a secretary of state he sounded like General Patton. His military background and attitude could hardly be concealed. He graduated from the US Military Academy at West Point in 1947, being placed two hundred and fourteen out of a class of three hundred and ten. By 1969 he was a Brigadier-General and rose to be a deputy-assistant to the president for National Security Affairs. Retiring from the army in 1973 he became assistant to President Nixon and White House Chief of Staff. He was recalled to the army in 1974 and became supreme allied commander in Europe (SACEUR) before retiring again in 1979. He was then named president of the United Technologies Corporation and, after giving up the possibility of being nominated as a Republican presidential candidate, he was selected by Reagan in November 1980 as Secretary of State.

He writes that on the way 'there was one passing cloud'[20]. He had noticed pain in his leg when playing tennis and a pre-employment medical examination connected with life insurance disclosed an obstruction in his coronary arteries although his examination on retirement from the army revealed no abnormality. He had had no serious illness although *Time* magazine later stated that an attack of chest pain in 1980 was attributed to indigestion. In late March 1980, according to Haig, Denton Cooley performed a double bypass operation at the Texas Heart Institute, St Luke's Episcopal Hospital in Houston. He continued to smoke cigarettes after surgery.

When his appointment had been approved by the Senate, and Reagan inaugurated, Haig's aggressive approach attracted attention. He was nicknamed CINCWORLD (commander-in-chief of the world) and accused of behaving like an assistant president rather than a cabinet member.

Early in March 1981 even the easy-going Reagan found that Haig's habit of pounding the table, and seeming ready to explode, worried him. Then there was Haig on the telephone 'going through the roof'[21] saying that he did not wish George Bush, the Vice-President, to have anything to do with international affairs. As the wounded Reagan lay in the George Washington Hospital on 30 March 1981 Haig rushed into the White House press room and told reporters that, in the absence of the vice-president from Washington, 'as of now I am in control here in the White House'[22]. He was apparently unaware that the speaker of the House of Representatives and the president *pro tem* of the Senate both take precedence over the Secretary of State in such a situation.

It has been suggested that after by-pass surgery some patients over-compensate and Claudia Wright, a journalist, quoted reports that over-stimulation of heart and circulation by prescribed drugs was also responsible[23]. Dr Christopher Bass, a consultant in psychological medicine, King's College Hospital, London, has given a professional opinion about the psychosocial problems which may follow coronary artery by-pass surgery. Type A individuals, and Haig with his hard-driving and competitive personality is certainly one, are liable to poor psychosocial adaptation, and 'are more susceptible to episodes of anxiety, anger and depression after operation than Type B individuals'[24].

Using Henry Kissinger's medical terminology, Leon Sigal wrote of Haig's 'glandular' foreign policy guided by his own metabolism and how, because he assumed that nods and winks from Reagan meant approval, he 'had a way of rearing through presidential signals like a runaway freight train'. Nods and winks are difficult physical signs to interpret. After real or imagined differences in 1981 Haig on several occasions offered his resignation. On 25 June 1982 Reagan gave Haig a letter accepting his letter of resignation which in fact he had neither written nor submitted[25].

During the Gulf War a picture appeared of Richard B Cheney, the US Secretary of Defense, and General Colin Powell, Chairman of US Joint Chiefs of Staff, flying to the theatre of operations with their feet up in a compartment of the aircraft large enough to have seated 20 ordinary passengers. In view of their health status envy or criticism should be stilled. Richard Cheney had his first heart attack in 1978 at the age of thirty-seven and, after two further attacks, what was described as quadruple coronary bypass surgery in August 1988; not, it should be noted, because it was surgically necessary but in order that he could continue backpacking and skiing. General Powell was on two medications for raised blood pressure[26]. Years ago they might have been regarded as invalid passengers and only allowed to fly after due approval from the airline's medical department. Two years later General Colin Powell, looking thoughtful, was photographed with Les Aspin, the new US Defense Secretary, who had to return to hospital to be fitted with a cardiac pacemaker[27].

Recent advances in cardiology are of no help to many patients. In 1965 Norman Kirk, then aged forty-two, was the youngest leader in the fifty-five-year history of the New Zealand Labour Party and, in 1972, the youngest Labour prime minister for nearly fifty years. In a two-year reign marred and fatally terminated by illness 'Big Norm' was conspicuous in opposing French nuclear tests in the Pacific and also visiting sporting teams from South Africa.

Weighing twenty-four stone his nickname was understandable but unexplained aspects of his medical history included so-called dysentery since his first trip to India in 1962 and a mention of goitre. He ate little, took unspecified weight-reducing tablets and, although he consumed excessive quantities of soft drinks, there was no evidence of diabetes. In March 1972 Kirk was experiencing cramps attributed to the tablets he was taking to reduce fluid retention. He often talked about death and, after attacks of exhaustion in October 1972, he was worried about his heart and consulted a doctor who said that 'one ventricle was not working as well as it should', but that his condition 'was not serious'[28].

The same doctor re-examined him a year later before an Asian tour, said he was in good health and, despite continued suspicion about diabetes because of his excessive thirst, there was no evidence of this condition while the problem with the ventricle had been righted. Nevertheless on 28 December in New Delhi Kirk went rigid, could not speak and seemed to be paralysed down one side. He recovered quickly and although he had pain on the left side of his head, slurring of speech and numbness in one leg, he made a good speech.

In April 1974 Kirk was admitted to hospital for varicose vein surgery which was complicated by a deep vein thrombosis, pleurisy and pulmonary infarction. On 2 May he was given anticoagulants, resulting a week later in epistaxis when he sneezed and either haematuria or melaena. One newspaper grimly summed up the position by stating that Kirk's deputy was 'a clot away from being prime minister'.

On 3 August Kirk had every reason to feel that 'something was drastically wrong'. He was apparently able to lead his party with vigour but offstage was exhausted, breathing with difficulty and complaining of 'dysentery' and drowning in his own fluid. Chest X-rays showed an enlarged heart and, since he refused cardioversion to correct an apparent arrythmia, he stated on 23 August that his heart was 'still fluttering all over the place'.

He was finally referred to Professor Tom O'Donnell on the 28 August who said he was not diabetic and any problem with a goitre was minimal. His heart was enlarged with an irregular beat and his liver was palpable. He was ordered to rest completely for six weeks while O'Donnell increased the dosage of digoxin to regulate the heart beat. His death on 31 August was attributed to ventricular asystole and the death certificate noted congestive cardiac failure for one month and thromboembolic pulmonary heart disease for five months.

Even from the incomplete details that are available it is clear that Kirk was gravely incapacitated and latterly bed-ridden in the final six months of his brief term, and there was ample evidence that, judged by standards applied to the average citizen, he was unfit to be prime minister in the first place. No doubt he wanted to fulfil his ambition while the Labour Party did not wish to admit that their leader was unfit to bear the responsibility of high office. Perhaps Kirk would have made the same choice again. For human and personal reasons his attitude is understandable.

A private citizen is only responsible to himself, his family and a small personal circle. Those in public life, who are disabled, must think, or be made to think, beyond their own or their party's ambitions. They often pay lip service to their duty to electorate and country. If they do not turn their pious words into action some mechanism must be employed to remove them from the scene.

'Common diseases occur most commonly' is the advice dinned into students or young doctors who presume to suggest an alternative to the diagnostic norm. As a result Boris Yeltsin has been misdiagnosed in the United States and Western Europe. The Russians have a tradition of heavy drinking but Yeltsin's main health problem is not alcoholism. Two Russian political exiles who returned to their native land in 1990 after thirteen years in exile have clarified the facts, half truths and disinformation of Yeltsin's medical history[29].

As a youth Yeltsin had what used to be a common form of heart disease in America and the United Kingdom. At the age of eleven in 1942 he was confined to hospital for four months with rheumatic fever, discharging himself by tying sheets together and escaping from a top-floor ward. It was a serious attack, because valvular heart disease was later discovered. By the mid-1960s, there were reported episodes of congestive heart failure leading to shortness of breath and swelling of his legs and ankles. His selection for Communist Party duties in 1969 provided ready availability of medical care and advice of which some was unusual. Certain KGB agents warned him that devices, operated from a distance, could produce impulses to stop his heart from beating.

There are other reports in 1988 of Yeltsin gripping his chest, possibly due to pain, and of a nurse supplying analgesics. Later he became suspicious of the Kremlin doctors and, after stopping 'a powerful hormone medication', his face became bloated and his condition deteriorated. It is not easy to assess whether Yeltsin's behaviour and competence are, or were, influenced by valvular heart disease stress or medication; perhaps by one factor, perhaps by a combination. His medical and psychological capabilities were certainly tested to the limits of normal capacity.

The extraordinary speech which he made at the Central Committee's Plenum on 21 October 1987 was attributed to him being incurably ill, suffering from terminal cancer, or even insanity. Soon after the annual celebration in the Red Square of the 1917 Revolution in November 1987 he was admitted to hospital because of a heart attack and nervous exhaustion. Two days later, when Gorbachev summoned Yeltsin to appear before the Moscow Party Plenum, his doctors gave him large dosages of tranquillizers and even sedatives. With slurred and incoherent speech Yeltsin retracted the criticisms which he had made at the October Plenum and virtually pleaded guilty. As a result at the age of fifty-six he was side-tracked to the non-political post of first deputy chairman of the State Committee for Construction.

Yeltsin fought back to be elected a People's Deputy in March 1989, chairman of the Russian Supreme Soviet in May 1990 and, having resigned from the Communist Party, Russia's first democratically elected President in July 1991. Despite this, during two visits to the United States in September 1989 and June 1991, the American press virtually accused him of alcoholism. On the first visit *The Washington Post* noted 'Yeltsin's boozy bearhug for the Capitalists'[29]. Such reports were later retracted but repeated during his 1991 visit when American newspapers referred to Yeltsin's liking for Jack Daniel's whisky.

The expectation of life and that of political power are by no means the same. Life may drag on interminably as a displaced leader reflects on his brief moments of power. Cardiac surgery can replace damaged valves while the risk of infected valves, bacterial endocarditis, can be prevented or, if infection becomes apparent, cured by antibiotics. In the short term Yeltsin's cardiac disease need not be a problem of the retention of power.

The medical history of Marshal of the Royal Air Force Lord Cameron should be a comfort to Yeltsin[30]. As a middle-grade officer, subacute bacterial endocarditis was diagnosed and, after a lengthy illness and an eventual response to antibiotics, he returned to duty in 1953 as an instructor at the RAF Staff College at the age of thirty-two. Although he was never again given a full flying category he became Chief of the Air Staff in 1973 and in 1976 reached the military peak as Chief of the Defence Staff, virtually the supreme commander of the British armed forces. An unwise reference to Russia as an enemy while on a visit to China led to the Chinese calling him a drunken hare—reminiscent of the remarks levelled at Yeltsin.

The cardiology of leadership cannot just be assessed on the mechanical damage and response to surgical or medical treatment. Sir James Mackenzie, the pioneer of British cardiology, for years a family practitioner in Burnley, Lancashire, reduced complicated instrumental evidence, guarded verdicts or obscure reassurance to simple terms; 'A heart is what a heart can do'.

Chapter 9

Too Old at Sixty-Five?

In his 1978 lecture on brain failure in private and public life Dr William Gooddy raised the question of a rigid retiring age, which is also relevant to a wide range of disorders acquired in later life outside the central nervous system. Certain professions and trades, he said, have a statutory retirement age 'perhaps to curb powers that may be impaired by the failing judgements and technical skills of later life'[1].

In contrast, some never have to retire and he asked what was so special about what is left of the brains of princes of the realm and of the church, great officers of the law, admirals of the fleet, field marshals, marshals of the royal air force, statesmen and politicians, that they never had to retire or, if and when they did, some years after the majority of the population.

Gooddy was following the old order of precedence when he put our Lords spiritual so high on his list. Even archbishops in Britain now retire at seventy, but in the past elderly clerics have forsaken the lobbying in the Lambeth conferences or cathedral closes and played a role, albeit behind the scenes, in national affairs. Nor is it so much a matter of their public condemnation of poverty, deprivation and frustration among the dispossessed and underprivileged which is criticized but rather an intrusion into political matters which should be none of their spiritual concern. Within living memory one elderly cleric was deeply concerned about a royal marriage and his judgement from on high was poorly received.

Cosmo Gordon Lang became Archbishop of Canterbury in 1928 and is now remembered for his alleged role in a conspiracy with Stanley Baldwin, the prime minister, in the autumn of 1936 to organize the abdication of Edward VIII, and for an unfortunate broadcast after the King had given up the throne and left the country. Lang's medical history is relevant as it later brought him into contact with Lord Dawson of Penn, consultant both to the King and Baldwin, who was also accused of plotting the abdication with Baldwin.

As early as 1904 Lang was advised to cancel a visit to South Africa as a doctor told him that his heart 'was showing signs of trouble'[2]. In 1914 Lang inadvisably spoke of his 'sacred memory' of the German Emperor and was deeply hurt by the depth and volume of criticism. This was the presumed cause of the complete alopecia which developed in 1916. In December 1928, just after his enthronement, he had sudden internal pain but his doctor and Sir Hugh Rigby, the consultant, decided against surgery. When Lord Dawson was called in there was still uncertainty about the cause of the pain but Lang understood them to say that a small clot of blood had wandered over his body and through his heart. Rigby added the hardly encouraging news that had they operated his heart would not have stood the strain. He had to rest for the next four months and it is interesting that as late as June 1930 Dawson diagnosed a duodenal ulcer.

In 1931 he developed trigeminal neuralgia and the pain was so severe that he was only capable of limited work, helped by Dawson's 'doping' that dulled the pain but left him conscious. The discomfort was improved by self-induced alternative therapy when he fell in his bath and struck his head so severely that he nearly lost consciousness.

At the age of seventy-two, he was in no condition to take wise decisions or indeed adopt a seemly religious detachment in the long-concealed and increasingly bitter struggle between crown, church and state over Edward VIII's proposed marriage to Mrs Simpson. In the early 1930s one of his chaplains described him as 'a most alarming and disconcerting person'. Lang was fearful of breakdown and drove himself to efforts which he would have been wise not to make. In November and December 1936 he saw Baldwin, who in turn had met the King on several occasions. However, Baldwin, shortly before his death in 1947, stated that Lang made no effort to force the issue.

It was his hastily composed broadcast, on Sunday 13 December 1936, which a man less over-tired and over-burdened might well have avoided or turned down, that is remembered for a striking lack of Christian charity. With the uncertainty over abdication removed Lang felt compelled to speak about the former King's surrender of trust for seeking his personal happiness 'in a manner inconsistent with the Christian principles of marriage'. Lang inflamed the damage by excoriating those in the King's social circle whose mores were contrary to the instincts and traditions of the people, and who should stand rebuked by the judgement of the nation. Lang was not only criticized for 'ungenerously exulting over a beaten adversary' but, while sitting in his car, heard Randolp Churchill shout, 'O, Cosmo Cantuar, what a cad you are'. A later, more irreverant and less God-fearing generation, might agree with the words of a lyricist;

> My Lord, Archbishop what a scold you are
> And when your man is down, how bold you are
> Of Christian charity, how scant you are
> And, auld Lang swine, how full of cant you are.

Nothing daunted, Lang conducted the Coronation service for George VI in Westminster Abbey in 1937 although Dawson, fearing the strain he would be under, sat in the south transept with syringe at the ready, prepared to inject at a signal from Lang's chaplain. As it was, Lang had to fiddle with the crown until it was the right way round, and omitted one prayer.

In the summer of 1941, aged seventy-seven, he decided to retire although in his view his bodily health was excellent and, despite what others may have thought, he himself was not conscious of any diminution of his mental faculties. He only took the step because at the next Lambeth Conference, possibly in 1944, he would be eighty, and too old to preside over discussions about the years ahead of that date. Lang died in 1945 at the age of eighty-one.

As for the great officers of the law, there is Hugo Young's alarming medical history of John Passmore Widgery who became Lord Chief Justice in 1971 at the age of sixty, resigned in April 1980 and died in 1981. Although his resignation appeared sudden he had been failing for the previous two years. His words in court could not be heard, he fell asleep on the bench and gave so few judgments that this task was left to juniors. It is understandable, but regrettable, that the legal profession closed ranks and either closed their minds in addition, or turned a blind eye to his failings. The Lord Chancellor, Lord Hailsham, was hesitant about taking executive action and finally Lord Denning, himself aged eighty-one at the time, took the initiative and Widgery retired.

Only at the eleventh hour did Widgery admit that 'he had suffered from a degenerative nervous disease for the past five years'[3]. One obituarist wrote that Widgery had Parkinson's disease and that he was 'obviously faltering under the strain and his resignation in April 1980 (the ninth anniversary of his appointment) was not unexpected'[4]. Judicial and legal colleagues can be justifiably excused on the grounds that they were unaware of the possible concomitant ill-effects of the condition which they may have understandably considered to be associated merely with rigidity or tremor.

Eight years after Widgery's death R C Baldwin and E J Byrne reviewed the psychiatric complications of Parkinson's disease. Cognitive impairment may be due to dementia affecting around one-tenth of these patients while two-thirds may have frontal-subcortical dysfunction which can cause 'slight forgetfulness, repetitiveness, and reduced initiative or creativity'. Depressed mood affects two-fifths of patients with Parkinson's disease but 'more common is a milder depression that is associated with motor disability', and is more likely if the motor symptoms worsen[5]. Such depressive pseudo-dementia is reversible and prompt treatment of motor symptoms can prevent it. Any psychotic disturbance is often due to anti-parkinsonian drugs.

On 20 July 1982 Lord Justice Ormrod, the third-ranking Appeal Court judge, who was in addition medically qualified, retired four years early at the age of seventy-one. Lord Denning, the

Master of the Rolls, also retired on that same day at the age of eighty-three. Two months before, a book which Denning had published was withdrawn after threats of libel by two black jurors, who had served during the Bristol riot trial in 1981. In his controversial book *What's next in the Law* Denning described how defendants, using their right of three pre-emptory challenges, could 'overload a jury with coloured people who were reluctant to convict their own'. The English were now white and black, coloured and brown, and 'some of them come from countries where bribery and graft are accepted as an integral part of life and where stealing is a virtue so long as you are not found out'[6].

Judging from the medical histories of certain justices of the United States Supreme Court, Lord Justice Ormrod set a pointed example to its members by his early retirement. With his medical background he must have been only too well aware that the chance of disability is considerably increased over the age of seventy. This is confirmed by the retirement of John Marshall Harlan, aged seventy-two, on 23 September 1971 because of a neoplasm in a lower verterbra. A short time before, the eighty-five-year-old Justice Hugo L. Black also had to retire because of a stroke and died on 24 September 1971. Doubts were expressed at the same time about the seventy-two-year-old Justice William O. Douglas who had been fitted with a pacemaker. Douglas had a stroke on 31 December 1974, returned briefly to the Supreme Court in October 1975 before retiring in November. He survived until January 1980. His trial run in the summer of 1975 in a local court in Yokima, in the state of Washington, should have precluded his return. For nine-and-a-half minutes during the trial 'he sat motionless staring at his hands and shuffling his papers without speaking'[7]. Fortunately he reserved judgment.

The British successors of the most senior judges such as Denning and Ormrod will still 'judge on' until the age of seventy-five. It can be argued that they work regular hours and their duties are limited by fixed legal terms and vacations. They may on occasion pass judgment on doctors who have to make instant decisions, involving life or death, despite the incomplete evidence from a changing clinical state. Judges, in contrast, can grant themselves the privilege of deferring both judgment and any sentence, while legal precedents are studied, which allows further time for reflection and decision. This is a priceless advantage denied to the harassed politician, military leader, business executive, surgeon or anaesthetist.

One law for the judges and another for the rest of the population is surely not just. It certainly gives rise to the inevitable caricature of an elderly judge, drooling on the bench, and asking, 'Pray, what is a sandwich?'. The octogenerian American judge, Joseph Buffington, had a name which might have been invented by Dickens, Trollope or even P G Wodehouse. He was retired at the age of 83 in 1938 having served as judge for the Third District (Pennsylvania, New Jersey, Delaware and the Virgin Islands). Not only was he handicapped by deafness, defective vision and senility but another judge, John Warren Davis, wrote and sold Buffington's alleged decisions in return for bribes. Davis was convicted and sent to prison but Buffington lived on until October 1947.

It is not only love of a profession or devotion to duty that keep judges and the rest of us at work long after sixty, sixty-five or three score years and ten. In his aptly named book *The Benchwarmers*, Joseph C. Goulden describes how the wife of a senile Texan judge was asked to persuade him to retire. 'What! And have him under my feet all day. Not on your life'[8]. The judge stayed on the bench and died in office.

Professions and trades are closed communities and members cooperate and even collude for reasons of self-protection against actual or potential criticism from the possibly hostile world outside. Familiarity, of course, can dull the recognition of change or even deterioration which may explain the delay in Lord Justice Widgery's retirement. The more senior the incumbent, or the more important his or her standing in a profession or occupation, the more difficult it is to broach the subject and attempt to rectify the position.

On 20 January 1993 the Chief Justice of the Supreme Court, aged sixty-eight swore in Governor Clinton as President of the United States. Yet on 5 January 1982 Justice William H Rehnquist, as he then was, aged 57 years, returned to the United States Supreme Court after admission to George Washington University Hospital on 27 December for treatment of what was described as a drug withdrawal reaction. Court observers had noted that the judge 'had difficulty speaking from the bench, sometimes mispronouncing words or pausing for long periods in the midst of questions'[9]. The hospital stated that he had temporary disturbances in mental clarity and began 'hearing things and seeing things that other people do not see or hear' after the drug, taken for severe back pain, was stopped.

When the drug, identified as Placidyl (ethchlorvynol) by *The Los Angeles Times*, was stopped there were withdrawal symptoms so the dosage was resumed and then slowly reduced. Ethchlorvynol dependence occurs on average after 1500 to 2000 mg daily for 60 days; 500 mg of this drug is equivalent to 30 mg of phenobarbitone. The *CBS News* commentator, Bill Moyers, echoed the views of many when he said that the secrecy was disturbing and while there could be sympathy for Rehnquist 'all of us are not justices of the Supreme Court'[10]. Nor would a majority in these circumstances even dream of becoming Chief Justice.

Justice depends on crime detection. From 1924 until 1972 the Bureau and, from 1935, the Federal Bureau of Investigation (FBI) in the United States was dominated by its director John Edgar Hoover.

There were dress regulations for his agents (G-men) who could not smoke or drink coffee on duty, while some were reprimanded for reading *Playboy* magazine. He served beyond the seventy-year retirement age and died in office on the night of 1/2 May 1972 aged seventy-seven years. In his opinion the longer an individual held office the more valuable he became, although by 1971 he dozed in his office in the afternoon.

Hoover had a minor heart attack in 1958 and his response to suggestions about diet and exercise was extreme. His death was attributed to hypertensive cardiovascular disease by the Washington DC coroner. There is no evidence of an autopsy and the diagnosis could just have been the opinion of Hoover's physician, who stated his patient had had mild hypertension for twenty years.

Hoover's experience was unrivalled but his disregard for contrary opinions led the Bureau to be involved increasingly with his own prejudices and suspicions, traits that worsen with age. Disproportionate attention was paid, for example, to surveillance of students, black or peace groups and even anti-pollution rallies. His bedroom bugging of the young John Kennedy in 1942 and, later, Martin Luther King may have entertained his confidants while inspiring fear that none would be spared.

Nor were all the secrets available to FBI staff or the Justice Department. After his death his long-serving secretary spent weeks destroying his private files, kept apart from the official records.

Hoover was unmarried, which caused comment about his private life. Furthermore his only close friend, Clyde Anderson Tolson, who had been appointed the FBI associate director in 1947, was also unmarried. They lunched and dined together daily, went to racetracks at week-ends and spent their Christmas break in Florida.

Hoover, like Churchill, showed another characteristic of ageing; the need to be surrounded by familiar faces. He showed poor judgement in retaining Tolson. Between 1951 and 1970, when Tolson reached the seventy-year limit, he was admitted to hospital eleven times for duodenal ulcer, repair of an abdominal aortic aneurysm, right and left-sided strokes, and complications of hypertensive heart disease. He was unable to shave himself or write with either hand. He survived his protective chief and died of renal failure in 1974[30].

In memoriam Dr Benjamin Spock, an anti-war activist and the people's party candidate for the presidency, called Hoover's death 'a great relief, especially if his replacement is a man who better understands democratic institutions and the American process'[31].

When Gooddy made the point that the most senior officers, the admirals of the fleet, field marshals and marshals of the royal air force, never retire and remain on the active list, he did not reassure the audience that they were rarely called back into active service, at sea, on land or in the air. On three occasions the results of the re-mobilization of admirals of the fleet, all interestingly enough on Winston Churchill's initiative, were not entirely happy or satisfactory.

In October 1914, despite the reluctance of George V to agree to the appointment, Winston Churchill, then First Lord of the Admiralty, brought back the seventy-three-year-old Admiral of the Fleet Lord (Jacky) Fisher as First Sea Lord. In his turn Fisher recalled as an adviser the seventy-three-year-old Admiral of the Fleet Sir Arthur Wilson who had been forced to retire from his post as First Sea Lord by Churchill in 1912.

The working habits of Churchill and Fisher were different, and possibly incompatible, but could at least have ensured a twenty-four-hour coverage at the Admiralty. Fisher woke at four in the morning, did much of his work before breakfast and went to bed at nine in the evening. Churchill, in contrast, woke late, had breakfast, worked in bed and then after lunch slept in the afternoon. Due to his mood swings his energy increased during the day and his most intense effort was displayed between 10 at night and one in the morning. Both temperamental and temporal difference caused increasing difficulty because matters which Fisher thought had been decided, when their work schedules overlapped in the day, were often altered by memos issued by Churchill during his night shift.

By May 1915 their relationship was clouded by disagreements over mining policy, Fisher's desire to sack incompetent admirals and, more important, over depletion of the Royal Navy in home waters to reinforce what was virtually Churchill's campaign in the Dardanelles which was not producing the speedy and successful result which he had envisaged and pushed through. As far back as January 1915 Fisher had reluctantly agreed not to resign and support the Dardanelles venture but on 15 May he resigned for the ninth time on the grounds that naval reinforcement of the Dardanelles exceeded the number of ships which had been agreed. His resignation was not initially accepted and, despite a signal on 17 May that the German High Seas Fleet was at sea, he refused to remain. He was bitterly criticized by Asquith, the prime minister, who did not accept his resignation until 22 May, and George V who said he should be hanged at the yard arm for desertion.

In assessing the resignation Churchill on the one hand played the part of an amateur psychiatrist. In his *Great Contemporaries*, published on the eve of the second world war, his opinion was that Fisher had a nervous breakdown and that his behaviour was due to 'hysteria, not conspiracy'. Asquith went further and wrote to the King that Fisher showed signs of mental aberration. On the other hand Churchill was not so charitable at the time and his attitude would now be condemned as racist. Due to his faintly oriental appearance it was always rumoured that Fisher was the son of a Singalese princess and a German naval attache, an 'unscrupulous (or cunning) half-Asiatic'[11]. It was also rumoured that he took drugs, an even graver accusation in 1915 than today[12]. On 26 May 1915 Churchill wrote; 'Fisher has acted like a treacherous devil. His Malay blood has come out'[13].

In November 1914 the forty-three-year-old Admiral Sir David Beatty, commanding the battle cruiser squadron, wrote to his wife: 'I honestly think that at the Admiralty they are stark staring mad, but what can you expect when they produce two old men over seventy years of age [Fisher and Wilson], who have no personal knowledge of the requirements and capabilities of a modern fleet, working with an ill-balanced individual like Winston'[40].

Conventional and often superficial tests of physical fitness should not be the only criteria for assessing individual capacity to serve after the widely accepted retirement ages of sixty or sixty-five. Unfamiliarity with changing structures of command, decision and action can cause disruption from frustration. Confusion is worse confounded when a senior officer from the past pulls rank and uses unofficial channels to further his doubtless worthy intentions despite the views of those now his seniors whom he still regards as juniors.

When Winston Churchill returned to the Admiralty as First Sea Lord in September 1939 he found an old map hidden away unused in the same room which he had left some twenty-four years before. It seemed his unhappy experiences with Fisher had also been forgotten as he recalled to active duty the sixty-six-year-old Admiral of the Fleet Lord Cork and Orrery. Since he lived until he was ninety-four an actuary would call him 'a good life'. Known as 'Ginger' Boyle he succeeded to the title in 1938 and possessed 'boundless energy, resolute offensive spirit and devastating fits of temper'[14].

After the German invasion of Norway in April 1940 he was summoned to the Admiralty by Churchill and appointed Flag Officer Narvik with the verbal understanding that the port should be captured. He had never met Major-General P J Mackesy, the military commander, whose written orders were different and equivocal about a prompt assault. It was obvious that the cautious, thorough and methodical Mackesy, ten years younger and junior in rank, would find it difficult to cooperate with his older, energetic, determined and impulsive senior, who to make co-ordination more complicated, was also senior to Admiral Sir Charles Forbes, C-in-C Home Fleet. Lord Cork had no direct authority over Mackesy, who refused an immediate assault on the grounds that adequately equipped and armed troops were not available because ships had not been tactically loaded and there was no mortar ammunition, artillery or landing craft. Cork had no written instructions and Mackesy's did not order him to attack at once.

Much of the forthcoming confusion resulted from Churchill who, as chairman of the military co-ordination committee, kept switching objectives irrespective of any practical considerations or limitations. On 20 April 1940 blizzards saved the troops from what could have been a disastrous attack. The combined operation was not facilitated by Churchill's instruction to Cork, now in official command, on 22 April that, if Mackesy was spreading a poor spirit, he should not hesitate to arrest him.

The fundamental difference was that Cork saw matters solely from the naval viewpoint, refused to establish his headquarters ashore and only late in April realized the Army's caution when he went ashore himself, was buried in snow and lost his monocle.

The unfortunate Mackesy had to hand over on 13 May, what proved to be his last command, to General Auchinleck who vindicated him in his subsequent campaign report. If he had given way on 18 April to Cork, an inferior force without snow equipment or weapons would have been dumped on snow-covered territory in open boats without artillery support. The operation was brought to a close when Cork received instructions on 24 May to evacuate Narvik as soon as possible. This created difficulties because it was not yet captured, and the objective of the unhappy Cork-Mackesy exercise was not achieved by Auchinleck until 28 May.

The third time that Churchill called up an Admiral of the Fleet from retirement he was also unlucky. In 1940 Sir Roger Keyes, aged sixty-eight, was well known and respected by Churchill as a fighting admiral. In 1915 he had struggled to ensure that the Dardanelles campaign should continue and, although many associated him with the daring raid on Zeebrugge and Ostend in April 1918, few remembered that the blockships were cleared from the former port after a short interval and never even reached Ostend. After his retirement he became Conservative MP for Portsmouth North in 1934. Right from the beginning of the second world war he used both his parliamentary and naval influence to criticize the conduct of the war at sea, demanded from Admiral Sir Dudley Pound, the first sea lord, 'more robust and resolute leadership'[15] and finally on 7 May in parliament, dressed in naval uniform, bitterly condemned the conduct of the Norwegian campaign for which Churchill was largely responsible. As a result of the debate Neville Chamberlain's majority on the motion was reduced to 81 and Churchill, after a chapter (of his) accidents, became prime minister giving Keyes, as a consolation prize, the dubious role of personal liaison officer between himself and King Leopold of the Belgians.

Whether Churchill was wise in appointing Keyes director of combined operations in July 1940 is debatable. He was thirsting for action and pressed for an attack on Pantellaria, an island between Sicily and Tunisia, in October 1940. This was postponed in December and abandoned in January 1941. He bombarded Churchill unsuccessfully with letters and demands for meetings until 19 October 1941 when he was relieved by Admiral Mountbatten.

Keyes' rise and fall in the second world war emphasizes the danger of appointing an older individual, who has held the highest rank or appointment in the past, to executive rank in a political, military or commercial organization in which he may be expected to defer to those who were once his juniors; while by directly approaching his former equals he breaks elaborate chains of command. Up to the end Churchill treated him with exemplary patience and consideration but when on 30 September 1941 Churchill had to remind Keyes that Combined Operations was not a private army, and that operations must have the approval of the high command, Keyes' reply ran to eight foolscap pages.

In his combined operations directorate Keyes struggled between the devil and the deep blue sea. The First Sea Lord, Admiral Pound, described Keyes as 'a perfect nuisance' and 'the only thing he cares about is the glorification of RK'[16]. In turn Keyes blamed the rejection of his schemes not so much on the chiefs of staffs committee but on younger staffs and inter-service committees unfamiliar with modern war. One obituarist of Keyes, Admiral W M James, wrote however, that 'his eagerness to strike at the enemy was not always tempered with good judgement' while his bold and imaginative plans 'may have held little promise of success or of making a definite contribution to final victory'. The too-bold admiral, as he was described, may have cut across chains of command in an effort to prove himself to others and to his own exalted standards of conduct.

The competence of those aged sixty-five years and over who continue in whole-time executive, as distinct from advisory or consultant posts, can properly be criticized on the grounds that in many, though not all instances, their mental and physical energy and capacity are waning. Although they may cite their varied careers and lessons learned, their defence can be countered by the reality that their experience is of events, decisions, successes and errors which are past history, and will never recur in the same way.

It is easy to be wise long after events but retrospective assessment is open to criticism because by then it may be impossible to question or examine the individuals involved. There is a responsibility, however, to future generations to ensure that tragic lessons from the past are not forgotten, and incorrect decisions leading to national and international disasters repeated. The mental and physical state of the American septuagenarian who abruptly broke off negotiations with the Japanese in November 1941 and of another, primarily responsible for the decision to launch the bomb and consequently the atomic age in 1945, should be seriously reassessed.

Cordell Hull was appointed Secretary of State by President Roosevelt in 1933 and by 1941 was confronted by diplomatic problems which would have daunted a younger, more energetic man. American and British diplomats in Tokyo were seeking a *modus vivendi* with the Japanese although both the American and Japanese armed forces were seeking time to mobilize. It is alleged that Roosevelt tempted the Japanese to strike first and that Churchill concealed from Roosevelt signal intercepts suggesting that the Japanese fleet intended to sail into the Pacific.

It was too much for Cordell Hull in his seventieth year and in poor health. He was off sick and out of Washington in July 1941 when signal intercepts revealed Japanese plans. Proposals about a settlement put forward by the Japanese as late as November 1941 were dismissed by Hull 'after tormenting uncertainty'[17] as unacceptable at a time when he appeared 'old, ailing, worn out by his exertions to reach a settlement'[18]. Later in November he sent the Japanese what they regarded as an ultimatum, an action described by Professor Julius W Pratt, his biographer, as 'a petulant one by a tired and angry old man'[18]. At what proved to be the eleventh hour on 26 November Hull responded to what were the minimum Japanese terms with maximum American demands.

Fifty years later Richard Lamb, a British historian, writes dispassionately of the events leading to that date which will live in infamy, 7 December 1941. From a British diplomat who was in Washington in 1941 he learned of Hull's loss of temper on 26 November which 'triggered off the Japanese attack in the Pacific; on such small things as a change of mood the course of history depends'[19].

Hull remained at the State Department until his retirement on 2 October 1945, his seventy-third birthday. When he died in August 1955 it was reported that he had diabetes and arteriosclerosis. These are common disorders and increase in frequency with advancing age, but do not entirely explain an unusual characteristic. Lord Halifax, British Ambassador in Washington, complained that the temperature in Hull's office was so high that it was like a greenhouse and made the veins in his head 'feel like bursting'[20]. When the foreign ministers met in Moscow in 1943 Hull had raised the office temperature to 90°F and Anthony Eden, then the British Foreign Secretary, thought he would faint. Dean Acheson also felt faint in Hull's State Department office and when an assistant said the temperature was 80°F Hull would say 'I thought so; let's have some heat'[21].

It raises the question of whether Hull was addicted to heat or had become acclimatized as do travellers from temperate climates when they settle in the tropics. It is possible that he had cold extremities from long-standing arteriosclerosis or that his susceptibility to cold was due to hypothyroidism, caused by reduced activity of his thyroid gland. Hull's incapacity remains debatable but the performance of those who met in his office was clearly impaired by the heat.

The other septuagenarian could have been selected primarily for political reasons. In the summer of 1940, when Roosevelt was considering the possibility of running for a third term, he appointed Henry L Stimson, a republican then in his seventy-third year, as Secretary of War, a position he had first held as far back as 1911. He

had also been Governor of the Philippines and President Hoover's
Secretary of State from 1929 to 1933. As early as October 1940
Harold Ickes, Secretary of the Interior, noted that Stimson was
mentally slow, far from alert and could only work efficiently for up
to four hours a day. Nevertheless on 6 November 1941, when
Roosevelt raised the possibility of a truce with Japan, Stimson
promptly objected.

In July 1944, when Stimson was seventy-six, the future Lord
Alanbrooke, then Chief of the Imperial General Staff, and a shrewd,
almost clinical, observer of Churchill and other leaders, noted that
Stimson was 'quite finished and hardly able to take notice of what
is going on round him'[22]. There was concern about his
cardiovascular system and his working days were reduced and week-
ends lengthened.

By April 1945 Stimson had to limit himself to policy questions
relating to the atomic bomb. As chairman of the Interim Committee
he advised President Truman on 1 June 1945 that the bomb should
be used. On 2 July 1945, however, in another memorandum to
Truman he stated he was in favour of giving the Japanese an
opportunity to surrender and the chance to retain their Emperor.

Just as Stimson himself had intervened in November 1941 and
objected to a temporary truce with Japan, now Cordell Hull, recently
discharged after seven months in hospital, advised his successor,
James F Byrnes, to omit any reference to the Emperor because it
was not only appeasement but guaranteed the feudal privileges of
the ruling class.

Two days after the first bomb was dropped on 6 August Stimson
proferred his resignation on medical advice, left the War Department
in September, had a myocardial infarction in October but survival
until 1950.

In 1947 Stimson had the grace to wonder whether a different
approach in May and June 1945 might have led to a Japanese
surrender without use of the atomic bombs. In the middle of June
1945 Stimson had retired to his house in Long Island for rest and
reflection. He therefore missed the last meeting of the Interim
Committee on 21 June when the decision to use the bomb was
confirmed and the die was cast.

Hull and Stimson had, in the past, been experienced and competent
administrators. By 1941 Hull at the age of seventy was exhausted,
out of touch with his office because of sickness, and unfit to take
part in delicate and rapidly changing negotiations. Stimson also had
the past experience, but came to the correct conclusions too late,
and omitted to attend the vital committee when his influence might
have delayed or avoided the decision to drop the two atomic bombs.

Forty years after the atomic bombing of Japan one historian, who
had tried to unravel the complexities of decision-making in the
summer of 1945, pronounced a verdict applicable to many who

remain in office after their 65th birthday: 'In the end Stimson had to content himself with maintaining the illusion of control while conceding much of its reality'[32].

The over sixty-fives have held commanding positions and responsibilities in past campaigns which the public and survivors from the armed forces regard as disasters. Recently, Eliot A Cohen and John Gooch have reclassified some of the more notorious as military misfortunes rather than disasters[23]. They suggest that those in high command are personally blamed although they may have presided over a military system in which the faults lie in its structure and communications for which, in some cases, the commander is not solely responsible.

They have studied five such military misfortunes and make a convincing case for their theory that the causes were failure to learn, failure to anticipate and failure to adapt. In two of the campaigns the responsible commanders-in-chief were over sixty-five and in a third he was in his sixty-fourth year. In the disastrous Gallipoli campaign on 1915 General Sir Ian Hamilton was sixty-two and Sir Frederick Stopford sixty-one. In only one of the five misfortunes quoted, the Yom Kippur War of 1973, were the commanders of a normally acceptable military age.

Although the two authors do not assess the mental and physical condition of the responsible commanders, and do much to lessen the slur of responsibility, failure to learn, anticipate and adapt can surely be expected and found more often in those over the age of sixty. Indeed this may be the reason, learned through bitter experience, that the fixed retiring age which has long been established in the armed forces is often lower than that found in civilian occupations.

If these three failures occur together they can be compounded by imprudent action or inaction by those in the chain of command leading to the catastrophic failure involving the French army and air force in May and June 1940. Two of the three failures occurring together constitute what the two authors called an aggregate failure which led to the defeat of the American eighth army in Korea in November and December 1950.

In September 1939 the sixty-seven-year-old General Maurice-Gustave Gamelin, the chief of the French general staff, became supreme commander of the French armies and also of the British expeditionary force. He may well have been one of those French leaders, criticized by the younger Colonel de Gaulle, 'as growing old at their posts, wedded to errors that had once constituted their glory'[23]. Gamelin failed on all three fronts of learning, anticipation and adaptation. He failed to act over the German invasion of the Rhineland in 1936, thought tanks could be neutralized by anti-tank guns and failed to establish proper cooperation between the army and air force. Even after the defeat of Poland in 1939, and the novel German use of tanks and dive bombers, he still relied on conscripted infantry. In 1940 he ignored his intelligence staff who warned him that the Germans might attack unexpectedly in the very place where they did—the Ardennes.

On the outbreak of war Gamelin established his headquarters in Vincennes, just outside Paris, devolved his responsibilities to other generals, and lacked control because of inadequate communications. He remained strangely passive during the Norwegian campaign of April 1940 and even after the German invasion of Holland, Belgium and France on 10 May 1940. When removed from command on 17 May his replacement by the seventy-three-year-old General Maxime Weygand says much for the current French faith in the military gerontocracy.

Cohen and Gooch charitably assume that Gamelin's failures to learn, adapt and anticipate arose because new information was 'not strong enough to break down existing preconceptions and presuppositions'. Apart from the understandable deficits due to ageing, there was possibly an even more serious and crippling medical cause for Gamelin's failure. That indefatigable medical detective, Dr Pierre Rentchnick, has discovered that in 1932 Gamelin had treatment in a French hospital, involving therapeutically-induced attacks of malaria, which at the time was the accepted treatment for advanced syphilis of the central nervous system. Needless to say, Gamelin's medical records were not available for inspection but a number of French physicians were still fully aware of the details after forty years[24].

Whether or not he had cerebral syphilis and responded to treatment is only one consideration. Even if his intellectual capacity was undiminished by infection it must be admitted that his passivity and indecision, almost amounting to evasion of responsibility, could have been due to inborn temperamental traits and failings inevitably worsened by ageing.

Neurosyphilis is less common now than in 1940 but a recent study poses the question whether Gamelin's mental state and reactions were affected by changes other than ageing. Of twenty-one patients with neurosyphilis referred to a psychiatric unit, sixteen had personality change, thirteen memory impairment, eleven hostility, ten confusion, ten hallucinations, eight expansiveness and four each had delusions and dysphoria[37].

Fifty years after the Anglo-French disasters in May 1940, Gamelin's culpability has been re-examined. Martin Alexander claims that Gamelin was impressed by German tank-aviation tactics in the Polish campaign in September 1939 and warned the Army staffs of the need for special training. Far from functioning in the isolation of what was in practice supreme Anglo-French headquarters, he kept in touch with and did visit his various Army commands. Alexander explains why the French generals under his command did not respond to what could be dismissed as suggestions as they were 'more often than not too old, lived on memories of the victory of 1918 and failed to show evidence of the activity we desired'.

The limitations of advancing age could have been a factor as Gamelin himself was sixty-eight in 1940 and General Alphonse Georges who held the key command of three army groups in North-West France was sixty-five in that same year. Suggestions had been made about a fixed retiring age of sixty-five years but application of such a change would also have resulted in the retirement of Gamelin. French generals incidentally were difficult to remove since many enjoyed individual and powerful political support.

Retrospectively Georges' failure and eventual collapse are not surprising. He had been wounded in 1914 and 20 years later was wounded again, this time in his hand and chest, when the King of Yugoslavia and the French foreign minister were assassinated in Marseilles. The German assault began on 10 May 1940 and by the 18th Georges was in a state of collapse. Whether he was too old to keep in step with the fast-moving blitzkreig, or whether his failure was innate, is difficult to decide. Yet one verdict is damning to Georges and can certainly apply to those normally regarded as pensioners. Georges' character 'showed itself not to be up to the high standard of his intelligence . . . right from the start of the crisis he was overwhelmed. He did not know how to organize his work, became submerged in details and exhausted himself to no avail'[38].

The seventy-year-old General Douglas MacArthur, despite his successful amphibious landing at Inchon on the west coast of South Korea in September 1950, has been blamed for the disastrous defeats suffered by his army in late November 1950. It was MacArthur, after all, who had pressed President Truman and General Omar Bradley, chairman of the joint chiefs of staff, for permission to send American as well as South Korean forces on the northern advance and, despite the risk of Chinese intervention, to bomb the bridges over the Yalu.

His reactions to the ebb and flow of active warfare were analysed by a number of unqualified psychiatrists. General Bradley, for example, blamed him for losing control both of the battle and his emotions and becoming hysterical, stupid or even mad. Dean Acheson, the US secretary of state, made a long-distance diagnosis in Washington on the basis of MacArthur's messages. He referred later in his 1970 autobiography, six years after MacArthur had died, to the latter's mercurial temperament, depressive periods, manic reaction and how he 'plunged from the height of optimism to the bottom of his depressive cycle'[25] and from that state to near panic.

Cohen and Gooch take a different view and consider that the failure of American leaders was 'fully to understand that the enemy's situation and their own bore little resemblance to those they had faced less than a decade before explains the debacle in North Korea'. They claim that it was an aggregate misfortune attributable to a failure both to learn and to anticipate. Both the political and military leaders failed to realize that their concept of a United Korea would inevitably lead to an aggressive Chinese response. Their misjudgment was compounded by their faith in air power, although the Chinese forces, unlike those of North Korea which had been trained and armed by the Russians, operated off roads usually at night, whilst their use of camouflage made them far less vulnerable to bombing.

There was also the failure of intelligence organizations to learn about and anticipate Chinese tactics. The blame can be widely spread but MacArthur, despite a distinguished military career, was surely too old and too senior to understand the novel techniques and attitudes of new enemies.

The massive sinking of American shipping off the east coast of the United States and the Caribbean islands in 1942 has been blamed on the sixty-three-year-old Admiral Ernest J King. Of the 650 000 tons of allied shipping sunk each month between January and September 1942, half or more were sunk in waters supposedly under American control. King bore some responsibility since, just after the Japanese attack on Pearl Harbor on 7 December 1941, President Roosevelt made King, who was then actually commander of the Atlantic Fleet, commander-in-chief US Fleet and later, in March 1942, chief of naval operations.

To Cohen and Gooch this was a straightforward learning failure so that no advantage was taken of British knowledge about anti-submarine warfare and the use of convoys, which was not instituted until May 1942. In King's defence it must be stated that there was a lack of escort vessels and aircraft, the Atlantic forces had been reduced to reinforce the Pacific Fleet facing even more urgent problems, lack of operational intelligence and, more blameworthy, absence of a black-out on the east coast cities and, finally, differences about the role of land-based aircraft.

On 23 October 1942 King wrote to Roosevelt informing him that on 23 November 1942 he would reach his sixty-fourth birthday and the official age for retirement. With the childlike facetiousness which passes for humour in great men Roosevelt wrote on his letter, 'So what, old top? I may even send you a present'[26]. King continued as chief of naval operations, where he was concerned with grand strategy rather than new and urgent tactical problems of a type better analysed and solved by younger men. Even at the highest level his alleged anti-British feelings, and preference for the Pacific rather than the Atlantic war, caused friction. On one occasion the equally hot-tempered General Sir Alan Brooke, Chief of the Imperial General Staff, nearly came to blows with him at an Anglo-American meeting. Brooke must have been unaware that when King graduated from Annapolis the title of his pen picture stood out from those of his classmates; 'Don't fool with nitroglycerine'.

There is not necessarily anything special about the brains, minds or bodies of those who struggle to become world leaders. Before

Mikhail Gorbachev's appointment in 1985 Richard J Willey, an American professor of political science, wrote of the 'elements of the Soviet pattern of power that made gerontocracy its natural form'[27]. A new Stalin posed the threat of early retirement for existing Politburo members only offset by appointing general secretaries 'who are aged and preferably ailing and who do not have the physical vigour to become genuine dictators'. Such an approach may be convenient to the select first eleven or fifteen in the Politburo, and even to the discreet inner circles of the democracies, where as Jerrold Post and Robert Robins point out, the disabled leader whatever his or her age, becomes the captive King of an inner circle of former courtiers.

Coming events cast their shadows before and in October 1980 Alexei Kosygin gave up the Soviet premiership at the age of seventy-six on the grounds that he had not recovered from a heart attack sustained one year before. His absence in early 1969 was attributed to a liver problem and in 1976 he nearly drowned after suffering a stroke while rowing on the Moscow river. His retirement was short and his passing an uncomfortable reminder to those addicted to medical check ups. Undergoing such a test in December 1980 he died when a nurse asked him to lift his shirt.

In January 1982 Mikhail Suslov, aged seventy-nine, described as the Stalinist ideologue in the Kremlin, died from a suspected kidney complaint and pulmonary tuberculosis. In view of Brezhnev's poor health it led western observers to speculate who in the wings would take his place.

Leonid Brezhnev admitted in November 1978, just before his seventy-second birthday, that he had had two heart attacks in the mid-1950s. In the previous year his health was of concern to Western officials during talks on strategic arms limitation. He had difficulty in hearing, used a hearing aid, his speech was slurred, he read from a prepared brief from which he did not deviate and no longer worked a whole day. On a state visit to West Germany in May 1978 it was noticed that his left leg was stiff, his face puffy and immobile, there was drooping of one side of his mouth, the large hearing-aid was obvious and there was talk of a pacemaker. A newspaper picture revealed him being supported by Gromyko and Chancellor Schmidt as he rose from a settee. There were further reports of his lack of spontaneity and inability to depart from a brief, that his pacemaker was made in America and that according to CIA reports he also had emphysema and gout.

By November 1981 there were reports of Brehznev's amazing recovery of health and strength due to reconstruction of his lower jaw and temporal bones which enabled him to speak more clearly. Plastic surgery can improve or at least alter the political image[27]. In the same year President Mitterand of France also had plastic surgery performed on his upper jaw to make it look less prominent;

whilst Chancellor Schmidt, who helped Brehznev to rise from a
settee, had plastic surgery to his face and a hair transplant. One
year later Brehznev died of a heart attack and an official report
stated that he had an aneurysm of the abdominal aorta, ischaemic
heart disease, coronary arteriosclerosis, and healed myocardial
infarcts. The pathology may be related to his habits because,
although he had an automatic cigarette case which ejected one
cigarette an hour, he chain-smoked between deliveries. Kissinger
once noted that Brehznev carried two automatic cases to increase
the cigarette supply.

On 1 February 1982 Michael Binyon, *The Times* correspondent
in Moscow, surveyed the contenders who with one exception, and
judged by actuarial standards, were hardly fit for leadership. Andrei
Kirilenko, aged seventy-five, and Victor Grishin, at sixty-seven, were
ill, Andropov was sixty-eight and Chernenko seventy, whilst Mikhail
Gorbachev, aged fifty-one, the one contender not geriatric was only
there because he had survived the hazardous agricultural post for
which there was no great competition.

Brehznev's two successors should shatter the all too common belief
that leaders, whatever their ages, are superior to those whom they
lead by reason of their greater endowment of intellect, physique and
ambitious drive to succeed and rule. His first successor in November
1982 was the sixty-eight-year-old Yuri Andropov whose position as
head of the KGB since 1967 must have figured prominently on his
curriculum vitae. Just before his sixty-ninth birthday in June 1983
he needed, like Brehznev, help in walking, sitting down and standing
up whilst his right hand shook uncontrollably. The likelihood of
Parkinson's disease was confirmed by Dr Pierre Rentchnick, who
has devoted part of his medical career to studying the invalids who
govern us. He noticed that when sitting at his desk Andropov's right
hand gripped his left, the usual method of checking tremor.

This is a serious disability for any individual in public life but,
in addition, there were reports of cardiac trouble as far back as 1966
and of a kidney disorder needing dialysis at the end of 1983. By
January 1984 Andropov had not been seen in public for five months
and his death on 10 February 1984 was hardly unexpected. The
official bulletin listed his various disorders as interstitial nephritis,
nephrosclerosis, secondary hypertension and diabetes mellitus all
'complicated by a chronic kidney deficiency'. The bulletin added that
'with the mounting phenomena of cardiovascular insufficiency and
the stopping of breathing, death came at 16 hours 50 minutes on
9 February 1984'[28]. Dr Y M Chazov, his personal physician, said
the patient's kidneys ceased functioning in February 1983 and that
he had been undergoing regular dialysis for the past year. In the
last two months of his life he was beyond hope of recovery and the
Soviet leadership had agreed that the seventy-two-year-old Konstantin
U Chernenko would succeed him.

Only a few days after Chernenko's appointment, Dr David (now Lord) Owen, who had a meeting with him in the Kremlin, said that he appeared to be suffering from emphysema. Television pictures of Andropov's funeral had shown that Chernenko was short of breath, wheezed as he read the eulogy, lost his place on several occasions and was unable to maintain a salute at the grave. Chernenko was known to be a heavy smoker and a western leader, after seeing him, made a gloomy prognosis, telling his ambassador that he would be attending another funeral during his present posting. At the end of 1984 Chernenko stayed away from the outdoor Red Square funeral of Marshal Dmitri Ustinov and was 'shaky and weak'[29] at a televised awards ceremony. In January 1985 a Warsaw Pact meeting was postponed and, when Chernenko failed to appear at a Kremlin election rally on 22 February, the Soviet people were told for the first time about his ill-health. Chernenko died on 10 March 1985 and Gorbachev, who as his chief deputy had been running the country, achieved supreme power at the age of fifty-four.

The West scorned the Chinese octogenerians while forgetting that Churchill stepped down reluctantly as premier when over eighty, while Konrad Adenauer only handed over the German chancellorship at the age of eighty-seven.

There was a dramatic shift of power in China in October 1992 when, out of the then fourteen-man Politburo, eight elderly members were replaced; President Yang Shangkun (85), Quin Jiwei (78) the defence minister, Wan Li (76) head of the National People's Congress, Song Ping (75), Yao Yilin (75), Wu Xuequian (71), Li Ximing (66) and Yang Rudai (66). At the same time the Politburo was expanded to twenty-two members, including a forty-nine-year-old but also, perhaps inevitably, the seventy-seven-year-old General Liu Huaqing, both regarded as reformers, as is Qiao Shi the sixty-eight-year-old head of state security[33].

Ironically, the changes were influenced by the eighty-year-old Deng Xiaoping the retired senior leader who 'remains the main power-broker and policy-maker because of his immense prestige in the military and the party'[34]. China-watchers noted that Deng's left hand was 'bent almost into a claw as it trembled violently'[35] and, although prompted and supported by his daughter, he looked frail and waved vaguely at the delegates. One wrist was wrapped in surgical tape leading to speculation that it had been prepared for an intravenous drip[36]. On television he was an admirable short-case for diagnosis but, whatever the extent of his brain failure in 1992, it was his intellect and psychological state in 1957 that must also be examined and questioned. Through his ruthless removal of hundreds of thousands of intellectuals from posts in the party and government in that year 'the brain of China was lobotomized'[33].

Where there is life, however, there is hope and Deng became the *Financial Times* Man of the Year for 1992, possibly because he defeated the 87-year-old Chen Yun in an internal struggle over economic reforms. Due to Deng, China now has a growing economy and in 1992 'the flowering of Chinese capitalism which he fostered became irreversible'[39]. Admittedly he was only an FT winner for 1992 and one of his predecessors is the deposed Mikhail Gorbachev.

Chapter 10

So What To Do Now?

Even those who have questioned, doubted or disbelieved the frequency and adverse effects of illness in leaders can no longer refute the evidence, they shift their ground. They adopt an aggressive defence and maintain that only illness and disability have been recorded without any attempt to suggest remedial action or solutions.

It is relevant that in the English-speaking world the main, if not the only, response to the problem of the sick leader has come from the United States of America. Such a reaction is to be expected from the most open society in the Western world and where the press and media benefit from the privilege of a right to investigate and publish. There has been condemnation of the yellow, tabloid and gutter press but the internationally respected American papers regularly publish medical details about presidents, senators, congressmen and others as part of their responsibility to keep the public fully informed. Perhaps it is for this reason that the false impression may be created that there is a preponderance of ill-health in American leaders. Medical information about British and European leaders appears less often; not because they are necessarily more fit, but because investigation is regarded as an invasion of privacy and newspaper proprietors and journalists have less justification to publish and be damned.

As far back as 1967 an American organization, The Group for the Advancement of Psychiatry, received a proposal for a research project entitled 'Stress and the Decision-maker'. Such an investigation was needed according to Dr William D Davidson, because the increase of agencies, bureaus and departments in the United States since the second world war had so increased the power of the executive branch that international decisions were made by no more than five men, and sometimes by the president alone. What particularly concerned him was the contrast between meticulous medical examination of, in this context, relatively minor decision-makers with the absence of any routine check on those at the top. He attributed this to the twin concepts of a 'national myth' and a 'hero myth' which, because of individual needs to maintain them, 'makes such an evaluation of our leadership appear as a threatening and even subversive suggestion'.

He listed some of the problems which should be the target of their investigation: increasing suspicion, irritability and resistance to new ideas, conflicting opinions due to fatigue, and the emergence of the 'inner circle' phenomenon when the leader is surrounded by a small group of devoted men and women. This results in a 'feed back trap' as the circle acquires and in turn reports back to their chief acceptable feelings and attitudes while filtering out unpleasant or critical messages.

In 1967 and 1968 Mottram Torre, a psychiatrist who for six years had been a consultant to American government departments and agencies at home and overseas, reported on psychiatric disability in high office[1]. At least some of his conclusions were also applicable to the effects of physical illnesses and, indeed, to the objectives of Davidson's proposed survey. Torre confirmed that less attention was paid to evaluating a leader's health before assuming office than to the state of health of minor officials or civil servants, adding that the demands on leaders may stop them receiving proper care, particularly for psychiatric disorders. As a result they may carry on when they have a grave physical or psychiatric disability and, more serious, colleagues of the leader may conceal the illness from the public. Leaders then become more dependent on certain associates whom they trust for emotional support and assistance at work.

Torre sounded a warning about the too-ready acceptance or tolerance of bizarre behaviour in charismatic leaders because, when they become irrational, their dedicated followers are blinded by devotion. He warned that successful leadership in some governments demands histrionic, violent and manipulative methods. Extreme expressions of emotion may be abnormal in one society but normal in another whilst in certain societies hostility, nationalistic megalomania and a belief in foreign plots are part of their everyday ideology and divert attention from domestic failure.

Professor Norman Dixon, a psychologist and former regular officer in the Royal Engineers, has made a classic and detailed study of military incompetence[2]. With regard to the dangerous leader, and his views can apply to the merely incompetent one, he admits the difficulty of any preventive action. Incapacity or abnormality is likely to be denied by the victim, subordinate doctors will cover up the condition and there may be fear of legal (and one might add lethal) action if the problem is disclosed. A further difficulty is the need and tendency for followers to believe in the physical and psychological superiority of their leader to maintain morale.

Dixon makes some practical suggestions about preventing the dangers of a failing leader. There should be more objective and realistic attitudes towards leaders whose physical and psychological strengths and weaknesses should be assessed by entirely independent physicians, psychiatrists or psychologists. His most controversial suggestion is that, in return for the perquisites and privileges of high command or executive office, leaders should submit to regular medical checks, even restrictions on alcohol, and conform to a fixed age for retirement.

Many conclusions of these older studies were explored in a more recent exposition of the psychopolitical dynamics of the disabled leader and his inner circle, described as 'the captive king and the captive court'. Jerrold M Post, a professor of psychiatry and political psychology, and Robert S Robins, a political scientist[3] confirm that leaders are as prone to illness as those whom they lead and, 'when the throne room becomes the sick room it can have catastrophic consequences for leadership, especially when the illness is concealed'. Intermittent or fluctuant disability is 'potentially most hazardous for the nation', especially if the leader denies or is unaware of disability; whilst the awareness of a fatal illness may actually force the victim into even more activity to achieve objectives. The dynamics of the inner circle are also examined by Post and Robins who suggest that, if the leader's illness leads to irritability, rigidity and wide variations of performance, the ability of the inner circle to control aberrant behaviour may be reduced and they themselves turned into 'compliant sycophants'.

In any country, whose leaders preach democracy and whose people think they live in one, those voted into high office should surely undergo the same medical checks and conform to the same retiring age as the voters. Airline pilots undergo six-monthly official medical checks and face early retirement although an error due to medical or psychological abnormality could at worst cause only a few hundred deaths. It is impossible to compute, and for faithful followers improper to consider, the world-wide casualty list caused by the economic, political or military blunders of a head of state and his associates. Leaders and their close advisers should be in the best possible physical and mental health and not beyond a recognized retirement age, however impressive their record may be. The latter requirement would probably be the most effective.

The establishment of an efficient and independent medical board to assess a head of state would be difficult. It is not just a matter of ensuring that the levels of blood pressure are in keeping with the average. Candidates are not in this case being examined for long-term fitness which is the object of pre-employment or insurance examinations. Nor are they being assessed for a specific occupational risk as with air crew or those exposed to toxic chemicals or radiation. Any comparable examination for political leaders would not only have to include their general medical condition but also their mental and physical resilience and reaction to the ups and downs of political life, internecine political friction as well as international problems, irregular hours of work by day and night and the excessive travelling which, because worldwide transport is available, cannot be avoided.

It is significant that in the United States the health of candidates only became an issue when Senator Thomas Eagleton had to withdraw as the Democrats' vice-presidential candidate in the 1972 election following the revelation that he had twice received electroconvulsive therapy for depression. In February 1976 and 1980 nearly every presidential hopeful agreed to an invitation from

Medical World News to submit a current and detailed medical report. Even the president, Gerald R Ford, then aged sixty-three, agreed. Rear Admiral William M Lukash, his personal physician agreed, albeit reluctantly, to answer questions at a White House press conference on 24 January 1976. Ford wanted full details to be given, which Lukash regarded as creating a precedent since only summaries of presidential health had previously been provided. Lukash objected to the release of medical trivia such as occasional rectal bleeding, nocturia (once a night), tobacco stains on teeth, small haemorrhoidal tags, brown and formed faeces, hyperaemic and friable anal mucosa, symmetrical testes and bilateral patello-femoral crepitation with chronic synovial thickening in both knees. Questioned about Ford's cholesterol level of 275 mg/dl Lukash replied that the normal range was 190 to 310.

Dr Lukash considered that such information should preferably have come from a medical panel and cited the difficulty of deciding the type of test and whether psychological ones should be included. He also asked, 'are we to turn down all candidates except those with perfect bodies?', since there are unmeasurable factors 'such as determination, wisdom, and inner strength that are more important'[4]. Some weeks before his opinions were made public John Sonneland, a Washington State surgeon, also recommended an independent medical investigation of candidates and, since mental testing is imprecise, recommended in addition for consenting candidates, an electroencephalogram and computerized axial tomography which would 'protect the public from some of the more serious brain problems'[5].

In the early stages of the 1980 presidential election the medical examination of candidates attracted both interest and controversy. The mixed, even contradictory, responses from 550 doctors polled by *Medical World News* indicated that there was no easy solution[6]. For example, although sixty-eight per cent believed that presidential candidates are owed from their physician 'an absolute obligation of confidentiality', fifty-seven per cent could conceive a diagnosis which they would make public for patriotic reasons and against the wishes of the individual. Of three hundred and fourteen doctors who could ignore confidentiality, seventy-five per cent listed a psychiatric reason, seventy-four per cent a disorder precluding completion of a four-year-term, sixty-eight per cent mentioned a progressive disabling condition and sixty-one per cent a chronic condition in remission such as nephritis or Hodgkin's disease. Some thirty-four per cent would break confidence for alcohol or drug addiction, cancer, cardiovascular disease, hypertension, venereal disease and potentially mood-altering drugs such as steroids.

The doctors in the poll were mainly opposed to revealing the details of the president's annual medical check after election and some sixty-five per cent said it was not necessary. This attitude is common to doctors in other countries and explains the secrecy over the illnesses of Roosevelt, Churchill, Eden, Kennedy and Lyndon Johnson. The doctors advising the Shah, Brezhnev, Andropov and Chernenko faced far greater accusation and penalties had they broken confidentiality.

Nearly eleven years later, in May 1991, the sudden illness of President Bush could well have been concealed from the American public and the world by, for example, the cover story of a virus infection. It says much for the keen eyes and ears of the American media, and their White House watchers, that the presidential advisers announced the nature of his disability from the beginning. They could not have anticipated that due to the persistence of the American press, of which Dr Lawrence Altman of *The New York Times* is an excellent example, not only were the White House press corps persuaded, or felt compelled, to give more details but every aspect of the illness, treatment, and side-effect of drugs were discussed by the leading endocrinologists and cardiologists interviewed by the media.

The clinical history was straightforward. Failing to take notice of Jimmy Carter's collapse when jogging, Bush indulged in this activity and developed a cardiac arrythmia which proved to be atrial fibrillation. Altman's regular bulletins in *The New York Times* between 8 May and September 1991 provide an excellent clinical record which lists the questions raised as Bush slowly responded to treatment. Between 8 to 10 May it was noted that Bush had lost three to four pounds in weight in recent weeks, and the arrhythmia was due to an overactive thyroid for which he had been treated with radioactive iodine. On 21 May it was disclosed that his thyroid had been overactive since the middle of April, some two weeks after his annual check-up. This did not include any thyroid gland investigation although Ronald Reagan underwent a T-4 thyroid function test in 1979. Next, and for the first time, it was asked how long the thyroid disorder had been present, in view of the possibility of hyperactivity before or during the Gulf War. Hyperthyroidism is well known to lead to shortened attention, snap decisions, frantic activity and fatigue.

On 22 May, two weeks after the diagnosis of Graves disease, Bush was given a clean bill of health although he had daily fluctuation of fatigue. Dr Lewis Braverman, an endocrinologist, commented that Bush was being given iodine drops which would decrease the levels of any thyroid hormone still present but would increase fatigue. Next day it was revealed that Bush had suffered more serious mental fatigue from the overactive thyroid and side-effects of drugs than had previously been admitted. Bush himself admitted to a slowing down of his mental processes and was aware that he was making mistakes, according to his physician, Dr Burton J Lee. Next day the latter admitted that a week after Bush left hospital, presumably mid-May, the overactive thyroid was 'accelerating fast' and Bush lost twelve to thirteen pounds in weight and looked and felt ill.

Every patient knows that for a period the treatment may be worse than the illness for which it has been prescribed. For those in any responsible position due thought must be given to the influence which the side-effects of curative drugs may have on them. In Bush's case cardiologists and members of some other specialities claimed that his mental and physical fatigue could have been caused both by an overactive thyroid and his subsequent mental slowness by the reduction in thyroid hormone in reponse to treatment. The thyroid specialists understandably blamed the side-effects on procainamide prescribed for his atrial fibrillation but Eugene Braunwald, a cardiologist, has never heard of mental slowing due to this drug. On 14 September it was reported to the media that, after Bush had undergone cardiac stress tests, his doctors considered him fit to consider re-election.

The medical history of President Bush which was revealed in May 1991 poses many questions. Doctors will ask themselves and each other if the diagnosis could have been made sooner. It is tempting, but possibly unhelpful, to speculate whether the worldwide travel and excessive jogging, golf and sailing indulged in by Bush were a manifestation of thyroid overactivity as well as an effort to overcome the fatigue it could cause, or merely visible activity to convince the American people that he was younger and fitter than his years. When asked in May why previous blood samples taken from Bush could not be used to determine his past thyroid function, it was explained that all samples are immediately destroyed by the Secret Service in case they get into the hands of foreign agencies. Sceptics had to be convinced that Barbara Bush's Graves disease, obvious because of her exophthalmos, and the lupus of their dog Millie, also an autoimmune disorder, were merely a coincidence. Although the water from The White House, Camp David and Kennebunkport was checked for iodine and lithium, which might have triggered an autoimmune reaction in the Bushes and Millie, the thaw in Eastern Europe ensured that suspicion did not focus on the disbanded or neutered KGB. It is still periodically suggested that the systemic lupus erythematosus from which Hugh Gaitskell died in January 1963 was due to a substance put into the coffee which he drank at the Soviet Embassy whilst obtaining an entry visa.

The medical care of heads of state involves the consideration of even the most remote adverse effect which, in a member of the public, would be unfortunate but would have no disastrous consequences to their countries and the world. For example, antithyroid medication has been known to cause a temporary schizophrenic psychosis in patients treated for thyrotoxicosis[7].

On 8 January 1992 Bush collapsed during a banquet given by the Japanese premier in Tokyo. The immediate concern was the possibility that the cardiac arrhythmia had returned. In view of his rapid recovery the convenient diagnosis of 'gastric flu' or 'a virus' seemed an adequate explanation.

The more suspicious turned to his past history which included the diagnosis and treatment of a peptic ulcer in 1960 and 1966. Furthermore, when he was in his thirties he collapsed with a bleeding ulcer in London, according to a report by Jeremy Laurence in *The Times* of London.

In the course of the dramatic faint that was transmitted round the world on television, one diagnostic possibility seems to have been forgotten. On 16 January 1980 Bush's blood pressure was 105/70 mm Hg which, in American and British opinion, is an enviably low level[6]. The German medical profession would disagree and treat low blood pressure which is defined as systolic levels below 110 or diastolic levels below 60 mm Hg.

There is no record of Bush's current blood pressure but the results of a British survey, published three days after his faint, showed that 'dizziness—giddiness in men and unexplained tiredness in both men and women were significantly related to low systolic blood pressure'[8,9]. It was concluded that 'there seems a strong relation between low systolic blood pressure and minor psychological dysfunction'. Nearly fifty years ago a leading British life assurance company would raise the premiums of those with 'low blood pressure'.

In June 1992 Bush was sixty-eight and later in the autumn the American voters had the power and responsibility to decide whether he would remain as president for another four years.

Some may regret that there is no precedent in Britain for the release of information about illness in prime ministers other than the misleading and uninformative bulletin of the type issued by Churchill's inner circle when he had his third stroke in June 1953 at the age of seventy-eight. The response of British doctors to the questionnaire sent to five hundred members of the American medical profession in 1980 might be entirely different, but surely a proportion at least would welcome the assurance that there is some medical check on British prime ministers. High standards of secrecy and confidentiality would obviously be available and vital in assessing a prime minister's health for his own and the nation's benefit.

The secrecy and anonymity of such a medical panel which would have every specialty on call, including psychiatry and gynaecology, would ensure confidentiality if a psychiatric opinion had to be taken. In 1973 Arnold A Hutschnecker, an American psychiatrist, asked 'what method of measures can we apply to evaluate the integrity or honesty of purpose and humaneness of a person who is about to enter a position of power in any branch of Government?'[10]. Concerned about the mental health of leaders for two decades, he had been attacked for stating that candidates, before any political race, 'ought to be cleared by a board of physicians and psychiatrists to make certain that they are healthy in mind and body'.

In the absence of a formal and professional assessment of candidates for high office, the more adventurous of the newspaper or magazine proprietors and their editors may lay themselves open to legal action and accusations of irresponsible and sensational publishing to stimulate circulation. What was considered to be a denigrating and malicious attack on, rather than an investigation of, Senator Barry Goldwater, the Republican presidential candidate in the 1964 United States election, is a warning against unrestrained comment about any individual. In the autumn of 1964 *Fact* magazine published 'The Unconscious of a Conservative; A Special Issue on the Mind of Barry Goldwater'. There was a twenty-two-page introduction by the publisher, Ralph Ginsburg, called 'Goldwater; The Man and the Menace', and forty pages devoted to the varied opinions of psychiatrists, some of whom remained anonymous.

The risks inherent in such an approach, whatever reservations there might be about a potential president, were made apparent in May 1968 when Goldwater, still a senator, took action against Ginsburg in a two million dollar libel action for false, scandalous and defamatory statements.

In support of Goldwater a pollster stated that only 2417 (twenty per cent) of the 12356 American psychiatrists had responded to the poll by *Fact* and of these 1189 found Goldwater 'psychologically unfit', 571 'did not know' whilst 657 considered him fit.

Goldwater's lawyer pointed out that even his client's feat in shooting the Colorado River rapids six times, donating ninety pints of blood, and personally flying seventy-five different types of aircraft, was summed up by *Fact* as a 'constant and irrational show of strength' and a masculine facade which fools people. There was some laughter in court which put Goldwater into a human perspective. Accused of sending a dead mouse along a pneumatic tube to the desk of a woman cashier in one of his Arizona stores, he replied that it was in response to her putting a dead scorpion in his desk drawer. At the conclusion of the action Goldwater was awarded 75 000 dollars as punitive damages against the already defunct *Fact* magazine.

If there is no official medical board to assess presidents or prime ministers, and even in America with its traditions of press freedom the press still has to be circumspect, a burden of responsibility to take action against a dangerous leader falls on the personal physicians. In most countries it is agreed that confidentiality may properly, even ethically, be broken if the conduct of patients is harmful to the community or themselves.

In the past, three distinguished British consultants clearly became concerned about their patient's ability to withstand the strain of office. In August 1936 Lord Dawson of Penn may have had nothing to do with an alleged or actual plot to remove the prime minister, Stanley Baldwin then aged sixty-nine, but he clearly considered him unfit to bear the burden. In 1952 Lord Moran discussed with senior officials the possibility of sending Winston Churchill, then aged seventy-seven, to the House of Lords, but remaining as prime minister, with Anthony Eden as acting prime minister for day-to-day affairs in the Commons. It would have resulted in the worst of both worlds and Churchill politely declined. At the end of 1956 dissent within his own party forced Eden, then aged fifty-nine, to contemplate resignation. Although there is no evidence that his physician, Lord Evans, played any part he was apparently aware of the intrigue and, far from supporting his patient, told R A Butler, a possible successor, that 'Anthony could not live on stimulants any more'[11].

After the British general election in 1992, John Major, the new prime minister, and members of his cabinet preached about the citizen's charter and the National Health Service. Health, like charity, begins at home. Surely they should display to the British public evidence of their own mental and physical fitness. The health of a public figure who presumes to lead the nation might one day, even in Britain, be a key election issue. So far as the electorate is concerned a public figure should not consider his health a personal and private matter.

Aspiring leaders should nevertheless realize that the road to disaster is also paved with good intentions. Paul Efthymios Tsongas, the former senator from Massachusetts and 1992 presidential contender, intended that a public statement should be made about his past medical history. A lymphoma had been diagnosed for which he was treated in 1986 by a bone marrow transplant, chemotherapy and radiation. When he entered the primaries for the 1992 election he asked for a full disclosure from the staff at the Dana-Farber Cancer Institute in Boston. With regard to an enlarged lymph node in the left axilla found a year later in 1987, it first appeared that the staff had only spoken of suspicious cells in the biopsy and that later radiotherapy was a precaution. Only after repeated requests by Dr Lawrence Altman of *The New York Times* was the axillary node pathology revealed to the Press; 'non-Hodgkin's lymphoma, nodular and diffuse, poorly differentiated lymphocytic type, or small cleaved follicular centre cell type'[12]. By that time he had dropped out of the primaries.

What could be called concealment was due to confusion rather than conspiracy. The medical team were certain that they had given Tsongas full information and he confirms this. In May 1992 he wrote that he and his doctors considered that removal of an axillary node in 1987 was a minor matter in 1992. His doctors had given him full details about the node at diagnosis and during later checks. They also wanted a full statement to be released in March 1992 but he was anxious to avoid possible difficulties between the Press and his doctors. He realized that he had made the wrong decision[13].

At the age of only fifty-one Tsongas optimistically looks to the future. If ever again he becomes a presidential or vice-presidential candidate he would permit his medical records at the Dana-Farber Cancer Institute to be made available to a medical panel entirely independent of the Institute.

He was echoing the view of William Safire who had personal experience of presidential responsibilities. In Nixon's first term he was one of the White House speech writers. Safire suggested that the way to avoid conflicts of interest, between patient privacy and public confidentiality, was for the Republican and Democratic National Committees to appoint a candidate's medical review board. He quoted a statement made by Tsongas on the previous day. 'Limited access to the record will no longer be an option for the future'[14].

It was a message that should have gone round America but clearly did not reach Governor Bill Clinton. If the jogging and sweating George Bush may not have wanted health and fitness to be an election issue, neither did hoarse Clinton. His reluctance to follow the example of recent presidential hopefuls and issue a medical report, inevitably led to speculation that he had something to conceal. In a ninety-five-word letter written in June 1992 Dr Andrew G Kumpuris, thought to be Clinton's principal doctor, stated that the contender's 'general health is excellent and his evaluation was totally unremarkable' although this was based on his last health check performed as far back as 27 August 1991[15]. No details were given about blood pressure levels or use of medications. Although Dr Kumpuris clearly stated that he would be pleased to give more information, he replied to a question by saying that it would be unethical to answer without Clinton's permission.

No doubt this prompted inquiry and led to hints that Clinton may have been treated for raised blood pressure. It is not clear why a student nurse should have taken Clinton's blood pressure during his campaign in March 1992 when a figure of 140/90 mm Hg was recorded, but attributed by Clinton to lack of sleep. Vigilant reporters had noticed that Clinton, aged forty-six, like Norman Kirk the New Zealand prime minister who died aged forty-nine from cardiovascular problems, drinks large amounts of water, leading to the suspicion that he was taking diuretics to lower blood pressure. In the same month it was also reported that he was on a low fat and low salt diet.

Although Sir George Pickering, a British physician, maintained that blood pressure readings were part of a continuum, and that there was no sudden cut-off point between acceptable and 'raised' blood pressure, a diastolic reading of 90 mm Hg in a man aged forty-six would surely demand further investigation in the health conscious United States. No conclusions, however, can be drawn from a solitary reading which should be put into historical perspective. When Franklin Roosevelt aged forty-nine decided to run for the presidency as early as 1931, one year before the election which he won, his blood pressure was 140/100 mm Hg. In the days when sedatives were the only treatment his levels ranged from a low of 136/78 in 1935, 188/105 in 1941 to 186/108 early in 1945 and figures of 170/88 and 240/130 in March and April 1945 just before his death[16].

What raised doubts about Clinton was Dr Kumpuri's statement that an exercise treadmill electrocardiogram had been taken. He gave no reason for this investigation which is puzzling, since the American Heart Association and the American College of Cardiology have reported that an exercise test 'is generally not appropriate in normal men without conventional risk factors'[15].

For many individuals a diastolic reading of 90 mm Hg at the age of forty-six may be of little significance if they follow a sensible life-style and diet. It does raise the question as to whether, even with the aid of modern cardiac therapy, such a theoretically border line reading can be sustained under the pressure facing a head of state in the world today. For four years, possibly, but the American electorate would be wise to ask the level of Clinton's blood pressure if he runs for a second term in 1996.

Whether or not the blood pressure of President Clinton represents a significant clinical problem, Americans can be reassured that he will almost certainly survive the four years of the first term. President Roosevelt objected to 'iffy' questions but, if Paul Tsongas' lymphoma had been publicly revealed before he won the New Hampshire primary early in 1992, other candidates would have been in a stronger position to challenge Clinton for the Democratic nomination[17]. If Tsongas had then been nominated, if he had won the election, and if the spin doctors had created a convincing cover story, the United States might have had a hairless president. If it had been disclosed that Tsongas had developed 'a new type of lymphoma'[17] necessitating admission to hospital and a course of chemotherapy, would he have had to retire before he took office? Or would there have been, as with President Roosevelt, carefully concealed visits to the Bethesda Naval Hospital?

The Summing-Up

William Somerset Maugham, physician, secret agent, novelist and playwright, once wrote that a story must have a beginning, a middle and an end. The beginning is easy, the middle enjoyable, but the end is daunting. It is often difficult to conclude any story whether fact or fiction. Yet Maugham's clinical skills applied to his analysis of human strength, failure and oddity, can surely be applied to the diagnosis and treatment of defective leadership.

It would be surprising if any individual with executive responsibility was not acutely aware of the possibility of sickness, stress or age-related failure among subordinates. What few are prepared to acknowledge is that they themselves are subject to inevitable mental and physical decline. Furthermore, it is often the precocious individual, the over-achiever, who may be unaware of the signs of premature ageing. To minimize this problem it would seem prudent to ensure that the 'all-powerful' relinquish executive, as opposed to advisory, responsibility before the age selected by actuaries as appropriate for retirement for the average citizen.

The media, if truly independent, have responsibilities in this field for they see, hear and observe the performance of political, industrial and military leaders and understand the machinations of their public relations advisers, courtiers and subordinates. Press and television staff and writers employed as political columnists should be selected for their interest, training, ability and conscientiousness to detect the earliest signs of irrationality or incapacity in those in positions of power. They should ensure, so far as possible, that their observations reach the public. Press censorship, overt or covert, may unfortunately frustrate the best efforts of the media from time to time and, regrettably, the public may ignore the diagnostic evidence provided. For similar reasons and as part of their training, members of the diplomatic corps, and civil and military leaders and ministers, should have the ability and interest to detect any aberration of behaviour or attitude. Neither the Hippocratic Oath (which most doctors no longer swear) nor the Official Secrets Act, signed by Crown servants, should inhibit comment on the condition of ailing, failing, criminal or dangerous leaders. Failure to act cannot absolve subordinates from responsibility and guilt for policies such as ethnic cleansing, unprovoked military action, mass destruction or genocide instigated by sick or psychopathic superiors. Unfortunately whistle-blowers frequently pay a heavy price for revealing information that is inconvenient for their superiors.

Regular routine medical examinations are required by some organizations but, as was shown in the case of George Bush, such routine procedures cannot prevent or predict the sudden onset of mental or physical illness. Some problems may be anticipated by the acute observers with detailed knowledge of the past medical history, the family history, and the environmental stress imposed on the subject. It is doubtful whether the subtle changes in stamina and intellect which accrue with age would be apparent to a clinician in occasional contact with the subject. Brain scans could indicate deterioration but it would surely be difficult to justify such tests to the 'all-powerful'. Further problems arise when leaders require surgery, whether it be for cardiovascular, respiratory or gastro-intestinal problems, trauma or, as with Reagan, following an assassination attempt. Recipients of the best and most lavish medical treatment, and the anxious attention of their subordinates and the media, these patients appear before the television lights apparently cured of their problems though in practice they may never again achieve their former psychological, mental, or physical capacity.

In theory, the vigilance of an observant press corps and the maintenance of the freedom to comment could be the best means of excluding unfit and incompetent leaders. Yet members of the press, public and political worlds may be guilty of the error for which Dr Watson was criticized by Sherlock Holmes; 'you see but you do not observe'. By the middle of 1994 it was clear from television pictures that President Mitterand, after a second surgical operation and chemotherapy, was unfit to serve until May 1995, his full term. The obvious illness of another French president, Georges Pompidou, was similarly ignored by the public until he died in office in 1974.

In the United States, measures have been adopted to reduce the possibility of an unfit president remaining in power. Limitation of presidential office to two terms (although some future president might bend the rules in a national crisis) penalizes the young as well as the old. Although Reagan was sixty-nine when he took office, the two-term rule still permitted an ageing, absent-minded and ailing president to serve until he was nearly seventy-eight. Conversely, the services of younger presidents could be foreclosed while they still have energy and open minds. Had Kennedy not been assassinated he would only have been fifty-one years old at the end of a second term while Clinton will be fifty-four.

The 25th amendment to the American constitution enacted in 1967 does not give any guarantee that a disabled president will be removed permanently, not just temporarily, from office. Only forty-eight hours after colonic surgery in July 1985, Reagan reclaimed presidential powers from Vice-President George Bush though he may well not have recovered from the effects of anaesthesia. This might account for his agreement, on the fifth postoperative day, to initiatives which led to the Iran arms deal. Furthermore, it is probable that his failure to recollect that agreement was genuine, rather than evasive, when he faced the Tower Commission in 1987. Bert Park, a neurosurgeon and trained historian, claims that the position could be remedied by the establishment of a Presidential Disability Commission staffed by carefully selected independent doctors and linked to the executive branch and the vice-president. They could use a system for assessing disability and impairment available since 1971, when the American Medical Association published *Guides to the evaluation of permanent impairment*[1].

By default, the one remaining means of lessening the risk of unfit leaders is the long-established fixed retirement age. This varies for both occupations and countries. In Britain it is illogical that senior administrative civil servants, who only advise ministers, have to retire at the age of sixty. The ministers, who may or may not follow their recommendation but bear the responsibility for political success or failure, are not constrained by any age limit. Based on actuarial experience, the retirement age for those with executive, distinct from advisory responsibility, in most occupations is generally between the ages of sixty and sixty-five. For world leaders crossing time-zones as a routine, forced to take decisions after long working days and disturbed sleep, the lower figure of sixty years is indicated and should be obligatory. At the age of sixty Harold Wilson was ageing mentally. The deterioration was obvious to close colleagues and even to himself for he resigned voluntarily as premier aged sixty. Whether the actuaries are responsible is not clear but the retiring age for women has, until recent changes, been set at sixty years. Had Lady Thatcher taken heed and retired before the 1987 election, when she was in her sixty-second year, she might have avoided the political errors of her third term and her humiliating dismissal by the Conservative Party.

There would be loopholes. It would be difficult to stop a British prime minister gaining office at the age of fifty-nine from serving one five-year term. Similarly, a US President, elected at the age of fifty-nine could not necessarily be confined to just one four-year term. If his party nominated him and there was no public objection he could run for a second four-year term which would last until he was aged sixty-seven. Politics may be the art of the possible but experience suggests that it should be made impossible for Presidents and Premiers to remain in office after the age of sixty-five.

References

Chapter 1
An Unsolved Problem

1 Kennedy, Alexander. *Lancet* 1957; **1**: 261-263.

Chapter 2
Ailing Leaders—So What?

1 Mortality Statistics—cause. Table 4 Series DH2 No. 13. 1986 Office of Population Censuses and Surveys, England & Wales. London: HMSO.
2 Health of the United States. 1989. US Dept of Health and Human Services. Health Status and Determinants. Table 26, 27.
3 Harmer, Michael. *The Forgotten Hospital*. Windlesham: Springwood Books, 1982.
4 Wilkinson, L. P. *Kings and Kingsmen, Kingsmen of a Century 1873-1972* Cambridge: King's College, 1981.
5 Jones, T. *Whitehall Diary*. Vol. I. Oxford: Oxford University Press, 1969.
6 Correspondence with E. G. Slesinger. 20 August 1972.
7 Johnson, Donald McI. *A Casssandra at Westminster*. London: Johnson, 1967.
8 Metropolitan Life Assurance Company Statistical Bulletin, July to September 1980.
9 Sidey, Hugh. *A Very Personal Presidency; Lyndon Johnson in the White House*. London: Andre Deutsch, 1968.
10 Busby, Horace. *The Washington Post* 17 August 1980. Review of 'Lyndon; an oral biography' by Merle Miller. New York: G. P. Putnam's Sons, 1980.
11 Rentchnick, P. and Accoce, Pierre. 'Ces malades qui nous gouvernent' and 'Ces nouveaux malades qui nous governent'. Paris: Stock, 1976 and 1980. Correspondence 19 September 1978.
12 Gromyko, Andrei. *Memories*. Translated by Harold Shukman. London: Hutchinson, 1989.
13 Altman, Lawrence K. *The New York Times Magazine*, 17 May 1981.
14 Rentchnick, P. *Médecine et Hygiène* 1982; **40**: 3546.
15 Shawcross, William. *The Shah's Last Ride*. London: Chatto & Windus, 1989.
16 Taheri, Amir. *Nest of Spies*. London: Hutchinson, 1988.
17 Sick, Gary. *All Fall Down*. New York: Random House, 1985.
18 Regan, Donald T. *For the Record*. London: Hutchinson, 1988.

19 *Time Magazine*, 22 July 1985.
20 Mayer, Jane and McManus, Doyle. *Landslide. The Unmaking of the President*. London: Collins, 1988.
21 *Tower Commission Report*. Bantam/New York Times, 1987.
22 Park, Bert E. *Politics and the Life Sciences* 1988; **7**: 50.
23 Wilson, William P. *Clinical Research* 1965; **XIII**: 7.
24 Henderson, Nicholas. *Mandarin*. London: Weidenfeld & Nicolson, 1994.
25 Alsop, Joseph W. with Platt, Adam. *'I've seen the best of it'*. (Quotation from Senator Charles McNary) New York: W. W. Norton & Co, 1992.
26 Evans, Rowland and Novak, Robert. *Lyndon B. Johnson: the Exercise of Power*. London: George Allen & Unwin, 1967.

Chapter 3
Do You See but not Observe?

1 Ober, William B. *Pathology Annual* 1970. Ed. Sheldon C. Sommers. Meredith Corporation.
2 Scott Stevenson, R. *Morell Mackenzie*. London: William Heinemann Medical Books, 1946.
3 Eisenmenger, Victor. *Archduke Francis Ferdinand*. Selwyn & Blount, 1931.
4 Pauli, Hertha. *The Secret of Sarajevo*. London: Collins, 1966.
5 Ludwig, Emil. *July 1914*. G. P. Putnam, 1929.
6 Agnew, L. R. C. *Journal of the History of Medicine*, April 1960.
7 Rees, J. R. *The Case of Rudolf Hess*. London and Toronto: Heinemann, 1947.
8 Moran, Lord. *Winston Churchill. The Struggle for survival 1940-1965*. London: Constable, 1966.
9 Barnett, Corrrelli. *The Royal United Services Institute Journal*, Summer 1991.
10 Boyle, Andrew. *Montagu Norman*. London: Weidenfeld & Nicolson, 1967.
11 Lock, Stephen. *British Medical Journal* 1984; **288**: 125.
12 Robitscher, Jonas B. *Cleveland-Marshall Law Review* 1968; **17**: 199-212.
13 Williams, Mark E. Correspondence 10 August 1990.
14 McEwen, J. M. (Ed.) *The Riddell Diaries 1908-1923*. London: The Athlone Press, 1986.
15 Vidal, Gore. *Collected Essays 1952-1972*. London: Heinemann, 1974.
16 Lewis, Anthony. *The Tuscaloosa News*, 1 November 1987.
17 Ritchie, Charles. *Storm Signals. More Undiplomatic Diaries (1962-1971)*. Macmillan of Canada, 1983.

18 Annigoni, Pietro. *An Artist's Life*, as told to Robert Wraight. London: W. H. Allen, 1977.

19 Beschloss, Michael R. *Kennedy v Khruschev*. London: Faber and Faber, 1991.

20 White, Theodore H. *The Making of the President 1960*. New York: Pocket Books Inc, 1961.

21 Jenkins, Roy. *A Life at the Centre*. London: Macmillan, 1991.

22 Woodward, Bob and Bernstein, Carl. *The Final Days*. London: Secker & Warburg, 1976.

23 Magruder, Jeb Stuart. *An American Life: One Man's Road to Watergate*. London: Hodder and Stoughton, 1974.

24 Dean III, John. *Blind Ambition. The White House Years*. New York: Simon and Schuster, 1976.

25 Brodie, Fawn. *Richard Nixon*. New York: W. W. Norton & Company, 1981.

26 Kissinger, Henry. *The White House Years*. London: Weidenfeld and Nicolson, Michael Joseph, 1979.

27 Kissinger, Henry. *Years of Upheaval*. London: Weidenfeld and Nicolson, Michael Joseph, 1982.

28 Blumenfeld, Ralph, the Staff and Editors of the *New York Post. Henry Kissinger, the Private and Public Story*. New York: Signet Special, 1974.

29 Hammer, Armand with Lyndon, Neil. *Witness to History*. New York: Simon and Schuster.

30 Blumay, Carl with Edwards, Henry. *The Dark Side of Power*. New York: Simon and Schuster, 1992.

31 Rowny, Edward L. *It Takes One to Tango*. McLean, Virginia: Brassey's US, 1992.

32 Shultz, George P. *Turmoil and Triumph*. New York: Charles Scribner's Sons, 1993.

33 Harsch, Joseph C. *The Christian Science Monitor*, 10 December 1981.

34 Osmond, Humphry F. Correspondence. 11 December 1981.

35 Woodward, Bob. *Veil*. London: Simon and Schuster, 1987.

36 Crowe, Admiral William J. Jr. with Chanoff, David. *The Line of Fire*. New York: Simon and Schuster, 1993.

37 Woodward, Bob. *The Commanders*. New York: Simon and Schuster, 1991.

38 Perry, Mark. *The Last Days of the CIA*. New York: William Morrow and Company, 1992.

39 Omested, Thomas. *International Herald Tribune*, 13 June 1994.

Chapter 4
On or Off the Record

1 Smoler, F. P. *The Observer*.

2 Farago, Ladislas. *The Game of the Foxes*. London: Hodder & Stoughton, 1972.

3 Bruenn, Howard G. Clinical notes on the illness and death of Franklin D. Roosevelt. *Annals of Internal Medicine* 1970; **72**: 579-591.

4 Moran, Lord. *Winston Churchill. The Struggle for Survival 1940-1965*. London: Constable, 1966.

5 Dilks, David. *The Diaries of Sir Alexander Cadogan, 1938-1945*. Cassel & Company Ltd, 1971.

6 Park, B. E. *The Impact of Illness on World Leaders*. Philadelphia: University of Pennsylvania Press, 1986.

7 Correspondence, Samuel M. Day—5 February 1970.

8 Correspondence, Samuel M. Day—13 January 1972.

9 Correspondence, Kenneth W. Warren—6 February 1972.

10 Correspondence, Robert M. Goldwyn—29 February 1972.

11 Goldsmith, Harry S. Unanswered mysteries in the death of Franklin D. Roosevelt. *Surgery, Gynecology and Obstetrics* 1979; **149**: 899-908.

12 Correspondence, William B. Ober—27 February 1972.

13 Lovell, Stanley P. *Spies and Stratagems*. Englewood Cliffs, NJ: Prentice-Hall, 1963.

14 Crispell, Kenneth R. and Gomez, Carlos F. *Hidden Illness in the White House*. Durham NC and London: Duke University Press, 1988.

15 Lake, Veronica with Bain, Donald. *Veronica*. London: W. H. Allen, 1969.

16 Massie, Francis M. *Modern Medicine*, 15 May 1961.

17 Correspondence, William B. Ober—23 September 1991.

18 McCune, William S. *Annals of Surgery* 1949; **130**: 318.

19 Anderson, Jack and Spear, Joseph. *The Washington Post*, 28 December 1985.

20 *The New York Times*, 15 October 1985.

21 Acheson, Dean. *Present at the Creation*. London: Hamish Hamilton, 1970.

22 Bradley, Omar N. and Blair, Clay. *A General's Life*. London: Sidgwick & Jackson, 1983.

23 Truman, Margaret. *Harry S. Truman*. William Morrow & Co. Inc, 1973.

24 *The New Republic*, May 3 1993.

25 Correspondence with Dr H. J. Dupuy in 1978.

Chapter 5
Brain Failure

1 Gooddy, William. 'Brain failure in private and public life' *British Medical Journal* 1979; **1**: 591-593.

2 Day, David. *The Great Betrayal*. Australia: Angus and Robertson, 1988.

3   Barnes, John and Nicholson, David. The Empire at Bay. *The Leo Amery Diaries, Volume 2, 1929-1945.* London: Hutchinson, 1988.

4   Bryant, Arthur. *Triumph in the West 1943-1946* (based on the diaries of Field Marshal Lord Alanbrooke). London: Collins, 1959.

5   Dilks, David (Ed.). *The Diaries of Sir Alexander Cadogan 1938-1945.* London: Cassell & Company, 1971.

6   Colville, John *The Fringes of Power. Downing Street Diaries 1939-1955.* London: Hodder and Stoughton, 1985.

7   Moran, Lord. *Winston Churchill: the Struggle for Survival 1940-1965.* London: Constable & Co, 1966.

8   Grizzard, Lewis. *The Tuscaloosa News,* 13 September 1981.

9   Buchwald, Art, *The Tuscaloosa News,* 13 September 1981.

10 Cannon Lou. *President Reagan; The Role of a Lifetime.* New York: Simon and Schuster, 1991.

11 Hoggart, Simon. *The Observer,* 3 January 1988.

12 Weinraub, Bernard with Boyd, Gerald M. *The New York Times,* 28 June 1987.

13 Stockman, David. *The Triumph of Politics.* London: The Bodley Head, 1986.

14 Wills, Gary. *Reagan's America.* London: Heinemann, 1987.

15 Hoggart, Simon. *The Independent,* 24 October 1987.

16 Cannon, Lou. *Manchester Guardian Weekly,* 28 December 1986.

17 Healey, Denis. *The Time of my Life.* London: Michael Joseph, 1989.

18 Pringle, Peter. *The Independent,* 2 June 1988.

19 Coen, Harry. *The Sunday Times,* 4 November 1984.

20 Personal correspondence, Dr Brian Butterworth.

21 Foot, Paul. *Who framed Colin Wallace?* London: Macmillan, 1989.

22 Persico, Joseph E. *Casey: From the OSS to the CIA.* New York: Viking Penguin, 1990.

23 Anderson, Martin. *Revolution.* San Diego: Harcourt Brace Jovanovich, 1988.

24 Gutman, Roy. *Banana Diplomacy.* New York: Simon & Schuster, 1988.

25 Doyle, Christine. *The Daily Telegraph,* 10 March 1992.

Chapter 6
Swings of Mood

1   *Time Magazine,* 1 December 1967.

2   Bradlee, Ben, Jr. *Guts and Glory.* London: Grafton Books, 1988.

3   Mayer, Jane and McManus, Doyle. *Landslide.* London: Collins, 1988.

4   Smith, Hedrick. *The Power Game.* London: Collins, 1988.

5 Persico, Joseph E. *Casey*. New York: Viking, 1990.
6 Wroe, Ann. *Lives, Lies and the Iran Contra Affair*. London: I. B. Tauris, 1991.
7 Connell, John. *Auchinleck*. London: Cassell & Co, 1959.
8 Bishop, Alan and Bennett, Y. Aleksandra. *Wartime Chronicle*. (Vera Brittain's Diary 1939-1945.) London: Victor Gollancz, 1989.
9 Harvey, John. *The War Diaries of Oliver Harvey*. London: Collins 1978.
10 Young, Kenneth. *The Diaries of Sir Robert Bruce Lockhart*. London: Macmillan, 1973.
11 Baker, Peter. *My Testament*. London: John Calder, 1955.
12 Rentchnick, Pierre. *Médicine et Hygiène*, 6 March 1991, p. 662.
13 Powers, Thomas. *The Man who kept the Secrets*. New York: Alfred A. Knopf, 1979.
14 Phillips, David Atlee. *The Night Watch*. New York: Atheneum, 1977.
15 Simpson, Christopher. *Blowback*. London: Weidenfeld and Nicolson, 1988.
16 Ranelagh, John. The *Agency. The Rise and Decline of the CIA*. London: Weidenfeld and Nicolson, 1986.
17 Pedrosa, Carmen Navarro. *Imelda Marcos*. London: Weidenfeld and Nicolson, 1989.
18 *Time Magazine*, 12 August 1991.
19 Bonner, Raymond. *Waltzing with a Dictator*. London: Macmillan, 1987.
20 Hougan, Jim. *Spooks, The Private Use of Secret Agents*. London: W. H. Allen, 1979.
21 Mangold, Tom. *Cold Warrior*. London: Simon & Schuster, 1991.
22 Taylor, Edmond. Awakening from History. London: Chatto & Windus, 1971.
23 Zumwalt, Elmo R., Jr. *On Watch*. New York: Quadrangle/The New York Times Book Co, 1976.
24 Tolstoy, Nikolai. *Stalin's Secret War*. London: Jonathan Cape, 1981.
25 Cannon, Lou. *President Reagan: The Role of a Lifetime*. New York: Simon and Schuster, 1991.
26 North, Oliver L. with Novak, William. *Under Fire*. London: Harper Collins, 1991.
27 Ljunggren, Bengt. *Emirates Medical Journal* 1991; **9**: 132-136.
28 Schwarzkopf, H. N. and Petre, Peter. *It Doesn't Take a Hero*. London: Bantam Press, 1992.
29 Atkinson, Rick. *Crusade*. London: Harper Collins, 1994.
30 Miller, Russell. *Sunday Times* Supplement, 13 March 1994.

Chapter 7
By Their Own Hands

1 Bohnert, P. J. In *Textbook of Family Practice*, 4th Edn. Edited by Robert E. Rakel. Philadelphia & London: Harcourt Brace Jovanovich Ltd, 1990.

2 Macintyre, Donald. *Fighting Admiral. The Life of Admiral of the Fleet Sir James Somerville*. London: Evans Brothers Limited, 1961.

3 Toland, John. *Infamy*. London: Methuen, 1982.

4 Newcomb, Richard F. *Savo*. London: Constable, 1963.

5 Hewitt, H. Kent. Planning Operation Anvil-Dragoon. *US Naval Institute Proceedings* 1954; **80**: 744.

6 Beesly, P. *Very Special Intelligence*. London: Hamish Hamilton, 1977.

7 McLachlan, Donald. *Room 39*. London: Weidenfeld and Nicolson, 1968.

8 Lewis, Nigel. *Channel Firing. The Tragedy of Exercise Tiger*. London: Viking, 1989.

9 Irving, David. *The War between the Generals*. London: Allen Lane Penguin, 1981.

10 Hoyt, Edwin P. *The Invasion before Normandy*. London: Robert Hale, 1987.

11 Rogow, Arnold A. *James Forrestal*. New York: The Macmillan Company, 1963.

12 Gromyko, Andrei. *Memories*. Translated by Harold Shukman. London: Hutchinson, 1989.

13 Correspondence with Dr William Sargant, 12 May 1967.

14 Bowen, Roger. *Innocence is Not Enough*. New York: M. E. Sharpe, Inc, 1985.

15 Crowley, Robert T. *The Daily Telegraph*, 21 April 1990.

16 Goldwater, Barry M. with Casserly, Jack. *Goldwater*. New York: Doubleday, 1988.

17 Beschloss, Michael R. *Kennedy and Khruschev*. London: Faber and Faber, 1991.

18 Halberstam, David. *Harper's Magazine*, February 1971.

Chapter 8
Hearts and Minds

1 Marriott, Henry J. L. *Annals of Internal Medicine* 1960; **52**; 411-427.

2 Friedman, Meyer and Rosenman, Ray H. *Journal of the American Medical Association* 1959; **169**: 1286.

3 Friedman, M. and Rosenman, R. H. *Annals of Clinical Research* 1971; **3**: 300.

 4 Groen, J. J. In: *Modern Trends in Psychosomatic Medicine.*
   London, Boston: Butterworths, 1976.
 5 Coffey, Thomas M. *Hap.* New York: Viking, 1982.
 6 Moran, Lord. *Winston Churchill; The Struggle for Survival—*
   1940-1965. London: Constable. 1966.
 7 Coffey, Thomas M. *Decision over Schweinfurt.* London: Robert
   Hale, 1978.
 8 Ferrell, Robert H. *Ill-advised.* Columbia and London: University
   of Missouri Press, 1992.
 9 Gilbert, Robert E. *The Mortal Presidency.* New York: Basic
   Books, 1992.
10 Clifford, Clark with Holbrooke, Richard. *Counsel to the President.*
   New York: Random House, 1991.
11 Perry, Mark. *Four Stars.* Boston: Houghton Mifflin, 1989.
12 Davidson, Phillip B. *Vietnam at War.* London: Sidgwick &
   Jackson, 1988.
13 Kinnard, Douglas. *The Certain Trumpet.* Brassey's (US),
   1991.
14 Maclear, Michael. *Vietnam; The Ten Thousand Day War.*
   London: Thames Methuen, 1982.
15 Karnow, Stanley. *Vietnam.* London: Penguin Books, 1984.
16 Kissinger, Henry. *The White House Years.* London: George
   Weidenfeld & Nicolson, 1979.
17 Schemmer, Benjamin, F. *The Raid.* Macdonald and Jane's
   Publishers, 1977.
18 *Bild*, 14 July 1972.
19 Jenkins, Roy. *European Diary 1977-1981.* London: Collins,
   1989.
20 Haig, Alexander M, Jr. *Caveat.* London: Weidenfeld & Nicolson,
   1984.
21 Reagan, Ronald. *An American Life*, London: Hutchinson,
   1990.
22 Persico, Joseph E. *Casey.* New York: Viking, 1990.
23 Wright, Claudia. *New Statesman and Nation*, 28 August
   1981.
24 Bass, Christopher, *British Journal of Hospital Medicine.*
   February 1986; p. 111.
25 Sigal, Leon V. *Survival.* May/June 1985, p. 142.
26 Woodward, Bob. *The Commanders.* New York: Simon &
   Schuster, 1991.
27 *Financial Times*, 18 March 1993.
28 Hayward, Margaret. *Norman Kirk.* New Zealand: Cape Catley
   Ltd, 1981.
29 Solovyov, Vladimir and Klepikova, Elena. *Boris Yeltsin.* London:
   Weidenfeld and Nicolson, 1992.
30 Cameron, Neil. *In the Midst of Things.* London: Hodder and
   Stoughton, 1986.

Chapter 9
Too Old at Sixty-Five?

1 Gooddy, William W. *British Medical Journal* 1979; **1**, 591.

2 Lockhart, J. G. *Cosmo Gordon Lang*. London: Hodder & Stoughton, 1949.

3 Young, Hugo. *The Guardian*, 2 July 1984.

4 Heuston, R. F. V. *Dictionary of National Biography*. Oxford: Oxford University Press, 1990.

5 Baldwin, R. C. and Byrne, E. J. *British Medical Journal* 1989; **289**, 3.

6 *The Daily Telegraph*, 26 May 1982.

7 Reston, James. *Kansas City Star*, 17 September 1975.

8 Goulder, Joseph C. *The Benchwarmers*. New York: Weybright and Talley, 1974.

9 *The New York Times*, 6 January 1982.

10 Barbash, Fred. *The Washington Post*, 8 January 1982.

11 Marder, A. J. *From Dreadnought to Scapa Flow*, Vol. 1. Oxford: Oxford University Press, 1961.

12 Rhodes James, Robert (Ed.) *Memoirs of a Conservative (J. C. C. Davidson)*. London: Weidenfeld and Nicolson, 1969.

13 McEwen, J. M. *The Riddell Diaries 1908–1923*. London: The Athlone Press, 1986.

14 Harvey, Maurice. *Scandinavian Misadventure*. Speldhurst, Kent: Spellmount Ltd, 1990.

15 Aspinall-Oglander, Cecil. *Roger Keyes*. London: Hogarth Press, 1951.

16 Roskill, S. W. *Churchill and the Admirals*. London: William Collins, 1977.

17 Feis, Herbert. *The Road to Pearl Harbor*. Princeton, NJ: Princeton University Press, 1950.

18 Pogue, Forrest. *George C. Marshall: Ordeal and Hope*. London: MacGibbon & Kee, 1968.

19 Lamb, Richard. *Churchill as War Leader*. London: Bloomsbury, 1991.

20 Halifax, Earl of. *Fulness of Days*. London: Collins, 1957.

21 Acheson, Dean. *Morning and Noon*. London: Hamish Hamilton, 1967.

22 Bryant, Arthur. *Triumph in the West 1943–1946; based on the diaries of Field Marshal Lord Alanbrooke*. London: Collins, 1959.

23 Cohen, Eliot A. and Gooch, John. *Military Misfortunes. The Anatomy of Failure in War*. New York: Vintage, 1990.

24 Correspondence with Dr Pierre Rentchnick, July 1978. Rentchnick, Pierre. *Médecine et Hygiène* 6 Mai, 1981.

25 Acheson, Dean. *Present at the Creation*. London: Hamish Hamilton, 1970.

26 King, Ernest J. and Whitehill, Walter Muir. *Fleet Admiral King*. London: Eyre & Spottiswoode, 1953.

27 Willey, Richard J. *The New York Times*, 26 February 1984.

28 Burns, John F. *The New York Times*, 13 February 1984.

29 Schmemann, Serge. *The New York Times*, 22 January 1985.

30 Gentry, Curt. *J. Edgar Hoover*. New York: W. W. Norton & Company, 1991.

31 Graham, Fred P. *The New York Times*, 3 May 1972.

32 Sigal, Leon V. *Fighting to a Finish*. Ithaca, NY: Cornell University Press, 1988.

33 Holberton, Simon. *Financial Times*, 17, 20 October 1992.

34 Pringle, James. *The Times*, 20 October 1992.

35 Sun, Lena H. *International Herald Tribune*, 21 October 1992.

36 Whitaker, Raymond. *The Independent*, 20 October 1992.

37 Roberts, M. C. and Emsley, R. A. *South African Medical Journal* 1992; **82**: 335-337.

38 Alexander, Martin S. *Fallen Stars*. Ed. Brian Bond. London: Brasseys (UK), 1991.

39 Nicoll, Alexander and Gowers, Andrew. *Financial Times*, 29 December 1992.

40 Ranft, B. McL. (Ed.). *The Beatty Papers. Vol. I 1902-1918*. The Scholar Press for Navy Records Society.

Chapter 10
So what to do now?

1 Torre, Mottram. *American Journal of Psychotherapy* 1968; October.

2 Dixon, Norman. *On the Psychology of Military Incompetence*. London: Jonathan Cape, 1976.

3 Post, Jerrold M. and Robins, Robert S. *Political Psychology* 1990; **11**: 331.

4 Altman, Lawrence K. *Impact*, 24 May 1976.

5 Sonneland, John. *American Medical News*, 8 March 1976.

6 *Medical World News*, 18 February 1980.

7 Bewsher, P. D., Gardiner, A. Q., Hedley, A. J., and Maclean, H. C. S. *Psychological Medicine* 1971; **1**: 260.

8 Mann, Anthony. *British Medical Journal* 1991; **304**: 64.

9 Pilgrim, John A., Stansfeld, Stephen and Marmot, Michael. *British Medical Journal* 1992; **304**: 75.

10 Hutschnecker, Arnold A. *The New York Times*, 4 July 1973.

11 Butler, R. A. *The Art of the Possible*. London: Hamish Hamilton, 1971.

12 Altman, Lawrence K. *The New York Times*, 28 April 1992.

13 Tsongas, Paul. *The New York Times*, 6 May 1992.

14 Safire, William. *The New York Times*, 23 April 1992.

15 Altman, Lawrence K. *The New York Times*, 10 October 1992.
16 Bruenn, Howard G. *Annals of Internal Medicine* 1970; **72**: 579-591.
17 Altman, Lawrence K. *The New York Times*, 17 January 1993.

The Summing-Up

1 Park, Bert. E. *Politics and the Life Sciences* 1988; **7**: 50.